I Gave Up Men for Lent

The story of a jaded, hopelessly romantic, health-conscious party girl's search for meaning

KACIE MAIN

Printed by B.C. Allen Publishing and Tonic Books

144 N 7th St. #525

Brooklyn, NY 11249

Now taking manuscript submissions and book ideas at any
stage of the process:
submissions@tonicbooks.online

Printed in the United States of America

Cover Design: Briana Simpson

Interior Design: Vanessa Maynard

ISBN: 978-0-9980299-0-0

Welcome to my life! My hope is that you can relate to some part of my story - a thought, question, fear, feeling, mistake. And in that, realize how connected we are really are.

Happy Reading!
Katie

TABLE OF CONTENTS

For all the men in my life—past, present, and future. Thank you for the love; thank you for the lessons; thank you for the material.

For my family and friends who must witness the sometimes devastating, sometimes incredible, sometimes comical story that is my life—I'm sorry, thank you, and you're welcome. I love you all.

There were several times during this process that the thought of putting so much of my life out into the world terrified me. Writing it down was one thing, but as I tip-toed down the publishing path and everything started to feel more concrete, there were many moments I contemplated turning around and running back to my normal life. But towards the end of writing my manuscript, I came across the following quote on Tim Ferriss's blog and decided to go for it and not look back...

The moment that you feel that, just possibly, you're walking down the street naked, exposing too much of your heart and your mind and what exists on the inside, showing too much of yourself. That's the moment you may be starting to get it right.
~Neil Gaiman~

WELL HELLO...

My name is Kacie Main. I'm currently 34 years old and I was 32 on the verge of 33 when I wrote the majority of this book. I have lived a very normal life... a great life by most standards. I grew up in Jacksonville, Florida with my wonderful family— mom, dad, older sister, and younger brother. I went to private school from kindergarten through high school. I made good grades, played sports, had friends, yada, yada, yada—no major traumas to speak of. I went to college, joined a sorority, partied my ass off, and somehow managed to graduate with a double major in Psychology and Communications with an emphasis in Public Relations. My career path post-college has taken some interesting turns but they've all been successful. I started out in PR, got into healthcare marketing, then healthcare sales, and then made an oddly sharp turn into the construction industry to be the HR manager for a commercial plumbing and mechanical contracting company. It was a random career move but the jeans and politically incorrect jokes were a breath of fresh air after years and years spent in the stuffy corporate world. I live at the beach, my friends are pretty awesome, and I'm now an aunt to a couple of the world's most adorable babies. Oh, and I got an MBA somewhere along the way. So yea—great life...

...until I realized I wasn't really happy.

Now how could I possibly be unhappy when, by most definitions, I lived a social, fulfilling life? Aside from the thirty-something and single combination, my life was picture perfect. But that was just a filter, like how the right Instagram filter can hide the dark circles under your eyes. The unfiltered me was restless... uninspired... uncomfortable. Something had to change and my history of failed relationships had me thinking my problem was men.

As you'll see while reading this book, I've been in love several times... not to mention some other fun, not-quite-as-serious male encounters. But each time, I ended up hurt. Each time, I was rejected. They didn't choose me... or so I thought.

Raised Catholic but not very religious, I still always liked the concept of giving up something for Lent. So when I drunkenly made out with a good friend of mine who had a girlfriend, and Lent was right around the corner, I decided to give up men. I added in a couple other things (sweets, hard liquor, and social media) so I wouldn't be "that girl who gave up men for Lent." I really didn't think much of it at the time. I just knew I felt negative about men and relationships in general and I wanted to remove that negativity. But as I put space between myself and what I thought was the root of my unhappiness, I began to uncover the fact that men weren't my problem. I was my problem.

Realizing this was no ah-ha moment. No wake-up in the middle of the night sweating. No collapse on the bathroom floor crying. It was a very slow progression of thoughts, an evolution of emotions, and a culmination of experiences. It was the beginning of acknowledgment for me. Acknowledgement that I wanted something different. Acknowledgement that I wanted something more. Acknowledgement that I was off track.

The first words of this book were written alone, at night, in my bed, with tears streaming down my face. It was just meant to be journaling—I needed to get certain things out of my head and onto paper. As I realized it could be the book I always wanted to write, I continued journaling and intentionally kept writing with that level of crying-alone-in-bed vulnerability. And I left it that way through every round of edits… despite the temptation to restructure it to fit a more normal/popular/commercial/mainstream storyline; or the pull to cut out parts that are embarrassing or feel pathetic, weird, or crazy; or the desire to spare people's feelings. I kept it true to where my heart and mind were in each moment.

My hope is that you'll relate and connect to some aspect of this raw, unfiltered account of what happened in my life and my brain during those 40ish days… and some of the 30ish years leading up to them. And in that connection, I hope you will find some peace knowing that you are not alone in your thoughts; or perhaps find inspiration to make sure you're living the life you really want. *Your* life.

If you're reading this book, that means I took a desire that always lived deep down inside of me, buried under all the *that's not possible* thoughts, and made it happen. And if I can do it, so can you. No matter what your deep desire is, it's possible. Don't think about the end result, the finished product, or the obstacles you think you'll have to overcome to get there. Just take the first step.

People always say you should pursue your dreams. But

before you pursue your dreams, you have to identify your dreams. And before you identify your dreams, you have to realize you are allowed to have dreams. That realization only comes when you take an honest look at your current reality—when you stop looking down the path laid out before you and pause to look at the options around you.

This book is ultimately about truth. Not so much being truthful with others but being truthful with ourselves. I think that's the hardest form of truth— to recognize and then acknowledge things about ourselves or our lives that are oftentimes easier to shove down deep inside. We all have truths like this. They reside in secret places within us. We don't talk about them with each other because we keep them hidden even from ourselves most of the time.

What do I mean by "our truths"? They are the thoughts we immediately push away, the questions we have but never ask, the things we want but don't fight for. They are the potential we aren't reaching, the feelings we aren't truly experiencing, and the person we really are... but lost sight of. They are usually buried under expectations we didn't set for ourselves and things we do even though we don't know why. They are buried under fear.

This is the story of me uncovering some of my truths. Yes, I gave up a bunch of stuff for Lent and you'll see how I was tested on it a bit throughout the 40-ish days... but what really happened is so much bigger. Each of those Lenten sacrifices were really just distractions taking up space. They—very successfully—kept my mind focused outward. When I removed them, despite it being a trivial decision at the time, I created space for my truths to surface; to raise their hands and beg to be seen. In the absence of all that external stuff to focus on, my attention went inward.

And so began a big change of direction in my life... what feels like a new beginning. My story is nowhere near over. I, like everyone else, am very much still figuring it all out. I'm just choosing to share my process.

I think we rarely share our process because it's messy... so messy it's hard to look at sometimes (just ask my family). It's easier to wait until we have everything figured out and then share our story as elegant experts who have already made it through the mess. I am still a work in progress and I have a lot of mess left to sift through. But I am committed to sharing my process in all its messiness because in today's world of filtering-your-life and posting-your-best-self, I think we could all use a little more messy and unfiltered... a little more real life. So heads up—this book is very raw (like #shitsabouttogetreal).

The most difficult part of this whole process has been recognizing that sharing my truth always involves other people and the truths they may not be ready to share yet. Or even confront. I really struggled with this realization. I knew I was okay with all the consequences of airing my dirty laundry—judgment, misunderstanding, maybe losing a friend or two or twelve. But airing other people's dirty laundry and forcing them to deal with the consequences? That's a whole other ballgame.

I believe we should all share our stories. I really do. Our raw, unfiltered stories. I believe so much good can come from it—connection, understanding, hope, inspiration. But I also believe that it should be done at your own pace. It's difficult to get to the point where you're ready to turn the dark corners of your mind, dig to the bottom of your heart, and deal with everything you uncover. I respect that process. It's no joke. I do not want to force anyone to do that before they are ready... especially in any kind of public forum. My story is my story, but I share chapters with a lot of people. Wonderful people who, like all of us, are just trying to figure out how to do this thing called life. I absolutely do not want to hurt, shame, or embarrass anyone.

I've done what I can to protect the confidentiality of the people who have played a role in my life while maintaining the integrity of my experiences. For the major past and current relationships, I used pseudonyms instead of real names and I've changed other basic identifiers. But thanks to the internet and years and years of Facebook stalking, we are all borderline private investigators at this point. So clearly, I can't guarantee you won't be able to find out who some of the "characters" really are. My ask to you is this—please don't do that. This is *my* story. The chapter any given "character" shares with me may not be the greatest chapter of their life but it doesn't define them... it's not their full story. This is simply my side of it.

I take full responsibility for every dubious situation I got myself into... and stayed in. I own the decisions I made and the decisions I didn't make. And as I sit here today, I am grateful for everything I have been through and I honestly do not regret a thing. Certain parts of this book come with a high risk of you judging me for my lack of regret. And to that I will point out that not regretting something is not the same as being proud of it. Am I proud of all the decisions I've made in my life? Hell no. But I now see that they were also the best lessons, my greatest teachers. It's the pain in our life that ultimately teaches us the most... not the great days at the beach.

So here we go—let's meet my truths and my teachers...

LEADING UP TO LENT: a storm's a'brewin'

2 0 1 6 - 2 0 1 7

AGE: 32

December 2016

I found myself not in a good place. Intellectually I was bored. My job of selling corporate health programs to local businesses, which once really inspired me, had become dull and frustrating. There was no clear next opportunity for me within the health system where I worked and I was pretty much sleepwalking around the office each day. I was job searching here and there but didn't really know what I wanted to do. It's hard to find a job when you don't know what you're looking for.

To add to my dissatisfaction, I had let an ex-boyfriend back into my life only to have him break my heart...

yet again. But it was different this time—I didn't really feel heartbroken. It was worse. I felt... bleh... an overall apathetic attitude towards my life and particularly the role men played in it. With my 33rd birthday six months away, I started to think that maybe I would never get married. Not in an "I'm a strong, independent woman" kind of way... more in an "oh woe is me" kind of way.

I just felt lost, like my life had lost its direction. Everything I had moved back home to Jacksonville for two years before—that (now ex) boyfriend and my job—had fallen apart. I had uprooted my life in South Florida—leaving my best friends, my job, my condo—for this new life in Jacksonville that was supposed to commence my happily-ever-after. And instead it had led to *bleh*.

If you knew me during this time, you would never have guessed any of this. Aside from a half-joking comment to a close friend or two, I kept my apathy and unhappiness all inside. The outside world saw Facebook posts with clever captions of me training for my first full marathon, taking random road trips, doing an elaborate Galentines Day Dinner with girlfriends, being "Aunt Kacie" to my first nephew, and by all societal standards, living a happy life.

And that's what's funny—by all definitions, I *was* living a happy life. My job was still technically a great job even though I was over it. I had a close family, great friends, a cute apartment four blocks from the beach, and an active social life. But still I felt off... like I was disconnected. Going through the motions but never feeling emotions. Just *bleh*.

I mastered the ability to trick everyone around me and even myself most of the time, but deep down I didn't feel happy.

Even though I avoided acknowledging it, the "off-ness" would rear its ugly head from time to time. On New Year's Eve, I was day drinking champagne with two of my best Jacksonville friends, Hadley and Rachel, talking about my job search and work in general. I commented that, "If you really think about it, what's the point of any of it? It doesn't *really* matter."

I went on to talk about how we just go to work to keep ourselves busy but essentially, it's all a waste of time because we aren't accomplishing anything in the greater scheme of things. "Most jobs are actually pointless—it's like we've overcomplicated everything to create busy work."

Okay. I can see my argument there but that's a *no bueno* thought process. If work is literally how we spend the majority of our time, and I'm saying that it doesn't matter... ipso facto, our time here doesn't matter? Truly happy people don't think like that. But I said it. And I meant it.

And then we finished our champagne, relocated to another bar, met some random guys, and accompanied them to a house party.

January 2017

I entered the New Year with a more positive mindset— that whole "New Year, New You" thing. My marathon training runs had gotten longer than I'd ever run. My Friday nights switched from playing giant Jenga at a local craft brewery to sober couch time and early bedtime so I could survive the long Saturday morning runs. I began to enjoy those nights in, waking up clear-headed and starting the day doing something active and productive. I began to feel a little proud of myself for tackling this goal, knowing how difficult it was going to be. Every time I completed a long run, it was like I felt a small breath of fresh air in my soul. A tiny moment of unadulterated happiness. I began to crave those tiny moments... almost looking forward to running 18, 19, or 20 miles in the cold on an early Saturday morning. Maybe it was runner's high but for me, it was more. It was hope.

I took a new approach to finding a new job... rather than actively search when I didn't know what I was searching for, I decided to start meeting and connecting with different people (I hate the word 'networking'), and telling them about my experience and that I was looking for something new. I took the "it's all about who you know" strategy. I reached out to old coworkers who had left to go to other companies, friends' parents who had big jobs, and even friends of ex-boyfriends who worked for cool companies. I just put myself out there more. From email conversations to discussions over coffee, I opened my mind to all kinds of possibilities that maybe my resume didn't lend itself to. And it worked, although not directly. I got recruited by one of my clients for what many would see as a very random career move—from healthcare sales to human resources for a construction company.

February 2017

I accepted the offer to join the construction industry,

an unknown world to me, to be an HR manager, which I had no real experience or knowledge in. I was set to start that new job just two weeks after my marathon.

So come the end of February, you would think everything would be better, right? Missions "New Job" and "Full Marathon" completed.

Well, not exactly.

I *was* excited about the new job—I knew it would challenge me to learn an entire new industry, new role, new everything. More than anything, it was a change. I couldn't sleepwalk around my current job anymore—I needed something to wake me up and I figured this random challenge had the potential to do just that. But I almost felt embarrassed to tell people about it, like being in HR wasn't a cool job. I had been in some form of health care sales working with doctors for so long. And in my more recent job, I had signed some pretty big deal companies in Jacksonville as clients. And now I was going to be in HR at a construction company? What would people think?

To top things off, completing the marathon was much more anticlimactic than I expected. I wasn't as proud of myself as I thought I'd be. I was actually disappointed I took as many walking breaks as I did during the last 13 miles. (In my defense, it was unexpectedly hot that day—especially compared to all my cold training runs... well, cold for Florida.)

I had so much support out on the course—my dad, mom, brother, sister-in-law, and even my sister-in-law's sister all popped up on the side of the road every couple of miles, cheering and holding funny, encouraging signs. My mother, Hadley, Rachel, and my friend April even joined me to run the last several miles. Other friends—ones I would never have expected such support from—came out to cheer me on and made signs. That part was awesome. But it almost felt like it was too much, like I didn't deserve all that support because what I was doing wasn't all that incredible. I felt the same way when I completed my MBA. Like these supposedly big accomplishments weren't really that big of a deal.

Why couldn't I really appreciate those moments of success? Why did I discount them? Why wasn't it enough?

At the time, I had no idea. What's worse than feeling unhappy in a happy life is not understanding why. Feeling like you *should* be happy because you have everything you think you need, but you're not... it's like guilt icing on top of your unhappiness cake.

JOURNAL ENTRY: jaded, *part 1*

MARCH 2017

I've given up men for Lent. I had the idea one night last week while lying in bed, feeling mad at myself for the stupid make-out mistake I recently made, but also sorry for myself because that mistake didn't want to be with me. I've just been feeling so negative about men and relationships and love in general. I want a break from all of it—

Is he going to text me?

Should I text him?

What did that text mean?

Oh, that guy is cute.

Should I make eye contact?

Crap, I didn't hold the eye contact long enough.

Check for ring on finger.

Damn, he's married.

There can't be a handsome, young-ish looking man within eyesight without me playing out some daydream scenario in my head about how we'll start talking, then dating, and then of course he turns out to be the man of my dreams. I mean, come on— just because someone walks into a yoga class with a decent smile and a penis doesn't mean we're going to hit it off. I'm just sooooooo tired of all the energy that goes into it.

My past is full of heavy, emotionally draining relationships. I've just run out of steam.

I wanted to give up something different this year— something more fun than sweets (which I've done countless times) or social media (which is also kind of overdone). I don't have many vices—I don't smoke, don't drink soda, and don't eat an excess of any one thing like carbs or cheese. Last year I tried to give up elevators, but then it was like every meeting I had was in a high-rise building. (sigh)

And then it hit me—men. Men are my vice.

I don't want to be that jaded girl who gives up men for Lent, so I added in a couple more normal Lenten promises—no sweets, social media, or liquor (not all alcohol, just hard liquor… ahem, vodka). My public answer is that I've given up "all the double-edged swords in my life" … things that cause me both pleasure and pain. That certainly fits my history with men—they've given me a lot of pleasure and caused me a lot of pain.

But my most recent pleasure/pain encounter… my drunken make-out mistake… was with a good friend. Arguably my best guy friend in Jacksonville. And now that friendship is in jeopardy. That's where I draw the line.

LOOKING BACK: crossing the line

2015-2017

AGE: 31-32

July 2015

David was about five years younger than me, undeniably attractive, and possessed many qualities I'm drawn to—namely, he was very driven and not so alpha male that he's a dick, but enough alpha that you know you won't win every argument. I met him about a year after I moved back home to Jacksonville when a recent shopping experience buying a larger pants size spurred me to check out a running group that met down the street from my apartment.

It's crazy how small, random, spur-of-the-moment decisions that seem inconsequential at the time can actually end up drastically changing the direction of your life. Walking down the street to meet up with that running group was one of those moments for me.

David organized and led the group. Running was absolutely his passion and he had found a way to make a living out of it—he worked at a local running store, organized running groups and local running events, and even coached people for long distance running. I remember when he gathered us around that first day to tell us the day's route—I took one look at him and thought to myself *are you f-ing kidding me?* I used to run with a group when I lived in Ft. Lauderdale and the leader was a large, ex-football player with a fantastically jolly laugh. And when I say ex-football player, think offensive line not quarterback. And then there was David—biceps you want to grab, dark brown hair, clear blue eyes, and just enough facial hair to tell you he's not quite as innocent as his baby face may seem. Now think quarterback. I rolled my eyes inside my head while smiling outside my head and introduced myself to him and the group. And so began our running relationship.

The running group was pretty close knit and we usually all grabbed a drink or dinner together afterwards. David and I clicked immediately. Nothing abnormal or sexually tense about it, but it was obvious we were similar in a lot of ways—very competitive, sarcastic, good hearts but twisted mind tendencies. From the beginning, we were able to talk and joke about very controversial topics. We often disagreed on viewpoints and our mutual stubbornness made for fun debates.

The most interesting thing about my friendship with David is that I've always been able to be very open with him... which is not my norm. Vulnerability is often an issue for me. But with David, I think it was just one of those fast friend connections.

I first became aware of it very early on in our running together when he asked me if I had a boyfriend. Totally normal question and one I'm no stranger to. As much as I like to think I haven't aged since I was 24, the mirror tells another story... and one that society (especially in "the south") doesn't really understand—I'm in my thirties and single. No, I'm not divorced. And no, I've never been engaged. Something must be wrong with me, right? I'm clearly either crazy or a lesbian. (eye roll)

I usually try to brush the question off by answering, "No, I'm not currently seeing anyone"—throwing in "currently" seems to make people feel more comfortable. They can rest easy that I do date... just not well. I then try to smile politely while suffering through the "he's out there, you just haven't found him yet" speech.

But when David asked me, I cut right through the bullshit. Mid-run I sighed and said, "Well, I *had* a boyfriend that I actually moved here for, but he ended up breaking my heart two months later, so nope, no boyfriend for me." I surprised myself by blurting out that personal, vulnerable information to someone I just met. Especially when I spent most days actively trying *not* to think about that whole situation.

Now before you continue thinking what I know you're thinking, know this—David and I were just friends. It never felt like anything else to me. Plus he had a girlfriend, Sara. She was young and sweet and would sometimes join the running group. He would confide in me a little about their relationship and reservations he had about it, but those conversations were always comfortably in the friendzone.

... until the first time I hung out with him outside of the running group... and he got drunk.

March 2016

David had been drinking while golfing with a friend

all day and they met up with me and my then-new-friend-soon-to-turn-boyfriend Adam afterwards to bar hop around the beach bars. I remember being surprised he was even coming to meet up with us— (1) because he's not much of a partier, and (2) in our almost year of knowing each other, we never hung out outside the group. It just seemed random. But we all bounced around the bars, playing games and trying moonshine flights, and everything was completely normal... until his friend went to the bathroom at the same time Adam went to go get more drinks from the bar. David and I were left at the table alone.

"I think I have feelings for you."

Huh?! I almost fell out of my chair. I immediately panicked and started looking around, like I was nervous someone else had heard him say that. I looked behind me and saw Adam signing the tab for the drinks. I looked back at David. He was so drunk that his eyes were barely focusing.

"Are those feelings re...cipro...cated?" he slurred.

I was still panicking. And I was pretty drunk myself. "No, no, no, don't go there—you'll ruin our friendship," I managed to get out right before Adam got back to the table with our drinks.

The night carried on like normal. David didn't bring the subject up again and I really tried to brush it off as drunk talk. I ended up hooking up with Adam that night which would jumpstart us dating for about six months.

David texted me the next day, apologizing for being so drunk and if he crossed a line or made me feel uncomfortable. I was excited about the potential with Adam, so I quickly dismissed the apology, saying it wasn't a big deal and he hadn't crossed any lines. It was never mentioned again and we both acted like it never happened. Then again, there's a chance he doesn't even remember it, so maybe to him it really didn't happen. But even if the alcohol stole the memory from him, his apology text proved he knew crossing a line was a possibility.

From that night on, I assumed David had a little crush on me but I always figured it was innocent—like a young boy having a crush on his older sister's friend kind of innocent. But still I tried to be very cognizant of not leading him on in any way.

December 2016

Fast forward eight months to this past December

when I was training for the marathon. At this point, David and I had become very close friends. Having completed several marathons of his own, he pretty much became my unofficial, free running coach. We didn't see each other outside of running together, but at that point we'd been running together consistently for a year and a half. If I added it up, that's probably more time than I spend with most people. We would talk about relationships and analyze life, and he consistently pushed me to question what good came from my booze-infused social life. I'd brush the conversation off and argue back that it was my avenue to let go and have fun and how my social life was important to me. And I meant it. Besides, I would still drag my butt out of bed before the sun came up to work out with a personal trainer at the gym *and* run at least once or twice a week. So clearly I had found a good balance.

David was an important element in my marathon training both physically and emotionally. He was supportive and encouraging and proud. He bought me a '26.2 in training' shirt and taught me how to tape up my shin splints. When friends or family complained about me staying in and not being social, he would always remind me I was working towards a bigger goal. And I needed that affirmation.

Admittedly, during that time I found myself sometimes questioning if there was more to our relationship than friendship. I would then question me questioning it, thinking *I'm just lonely*. It was a matter I never really gave much attention to, dismissing it for a variety of reasons—*he's just a friend, he's too young, he has a girlfriend*. I didn't allow myself to think about it too much and instead just remained focused on my training.

February 2017

And now we're back up to this year—only a couple weeks before Lent. I just finished the marathon and was in my last week at my corporate health job, about to start my new job.

The weekend after the marathon, David asked if I wanted to go out to the beach bars with him—a friend of his was in town and she wanted him to hang out. He didn't really want to go out, but he felt pressured to hang out with this friend and he knew I was no stranger to that scene. So he recruited me for moral support since Sara was out of town.

I agreed to go out with him even though I felt a little uneasy about it, largely due to Sara. David had admitted to me that she had some jealousy issues regarding our friendship—apparently rightfully so—when they first got together. But for the most part, she had gotten over it and according to David, now "looks up to me." (cringe)

Something existed in the planning conversations that didn't feel 100% friendzone. And not just from his end. The questions about the true nature of my feelings for him had started to creep back into my mind. I kept pushing them away but they kept popping up.

He offered to pick me up because my place was on the way to the beach bars. I definitely didn't feel comfortable riding in his car. Maybe because being picked up felt too date-like and that felt unnatural with him. Maybe because I knew it was wrong on some level, knowing Sara would not be pleased with the scene. Or maybe it was because I was legit nervous... like first-date nervous. Maybe all the above.

It was clear from the first bar that he was on a mission to get drunk. I, on the other hand, was on a mission to keep my drinking under control for fear that drunken Kacie—who also happened to be lonely and still trying to overcome feelings of rejection from my most recent heartbreak—would want to explore the questions about my feelings for David...

likely in a physical manner. I told myself over and over again before he picked me up that nothing was going to happen. He had a girlfriend and I absolutely did not want to disrespect her. Plus I really valued our friendship and didn't want to put it at risk just because I was desperate for someone to want me.

We met up with his friend and as the night went on, I could see him getting drunker and drunker. I'd like to say I succeeded in keeping my own drinking under control but that wouldn't be the entire truth. As the drinks flowed, his guard came down and I'd catch him looking at me and smiling in a way I'd never seen before. And in my Fireball-shots-unguarded-state, my gut reaction to those looks was my answer—uncomfortable. Something just didn't feel right.

And just like that, all the questions I had about my feelings for him seemed to disappear. I remember looking at him and thinking *yep, just friends*. And I meant it. It was a moment of somewhat drunken clarity.

A couple of blurry hours later, we were standing next to his car. He was hammered and I was trying to pry the keys out of his hand so he wouldn't drive home. I finally succeeded and hit the Uber button on my phone. When we got in the Uber, I asked him, "What's your address?"

No, I wasn't planning to go home with him. I was going to have Uber drop him off and then take me home. It was an innocent plan... until he refused to give the driver his address.

His hopeful eyes watched me. "We're going to my place?"

"No. We are dropping you off at your place and then he's driving me home." I said it with strong conviction. I meant it.

"No," is all he would then say and shake his head. While David is a bit of an old soul, drunken David shows his true age. Maybe even younger. This conversation was like trying to tell an unruly toddler to eat his peas and all he'd do was close his eyes, tilt his head up, and shake it back and forth.

I tried and I tried but I couldn't get his address out of him. Thinking back on it, I realize I should have reached into his pocket and stolen his wallet to look at his license. Ugh—hindsight.

"Fine," I said, giving up. "You can sleep on my couch and I'll take you to your car in the morning."

We walked into my apartment and he sat down on the couch. I should have given him a blanket and immediately retreated upstairs to my bedroom. Instead I sat down too.

I can't say I clearly remember our conversation but I know it got real. I remember squirming uncomfortably as he told me how impressed he was with me, from my body to my wit, determination, and brain. I remember worrying he wasn't really hearing me as I tried to explain why I thought we were meant to just be friends. And I remember him telling me he thought he was in love with me for the past two years. *Love.* I hadn't seen that coming. The word touched something in my heart that hadn't been touched in a while. I remember going back and forth in my head about how to respond. And I remember the exact moment when I decided to cave... to not care... and I leaned over and kissed him.

The make-out session that ensued was nothing short of hot. Our lips and tongues moved in sync and his hands explored my body like he had mapped it out in his mind over and over again. I felt wanted. I felt sexy. I felt alive.

He picked me up off the couch and laid me down on my back. Kneeling over me, he took his shirt off and as he began to lean back down into another kiss... the kiss that would propel the situation to a point of no return... I suddenly came to my senses. My hand went up against his bare chest and I pushed him away.

"Stop," I said. "We can't do this."

My mind was racing... *I don't want this... It feels so good to be touched... It's not right... Who cares?*

My living room turned into a movie-like scene of me slowly convincing him to Uber home, oscillating between pushing him towards the door and collapsing into his arms for another kiss. All the while seriously debating just saying "F it" and ripping his clothes off. The number one reason I didn't was Sara. She didn't deserve this. And I didn't want to be *that* girl, the other woman. I'd been her before.

(That's another story for another time.)

The scene came to a close and he finally left.

The next morning I texted him to see if he was okay. He responded saying he was hungover and asked how I was feeling. When I replied that I was okay but feeling a little guilty, he quickly texted back, "Don't. I don't want to talk about it." I wasn't entirely sure what emotions were behind that curt demand—perhaps he was angry with himself for disrespecting Sara. Or maybe he felt rejected from having dropped the L bomb and me not reciprocating. Or maybe he didn't remember much but knew enough from reading back through his text messages—all of which were asking me to come over after he finally got home—and he was embarrassed.

The rest of the weekend I went on an analytical roller coaster over what happened, how I felt about it, and what it all meant. I would swing from being angry with myself for making such a stupid drunken mistake with a friend, to again thinking maybe there was something more between us. Was my supposed moment of drunken clarity more 'drunken' or more 'clarity'? I tried to picture my life with him, wondering if I would be happy long-term with someone who didn't fit the "on paper" description of what I was looking for—David was younger than me, and didn't have a corporate America, white collar, "real job" like I always expected my ideal husband would have. I honestly didn't know how I felt or what I wanted and it was frustrating. All I knew was that I didn't want to force myself in either direction—I didn't want to assume there was more between us if I was really just lonely and desperately wanting someone to want me after my ex had once again rejected me; and I didn't want to discount the possibility of something more for trivial reasons or because I was so jaded from all of my previous relationships.

At work on Monday morning I talked to my coworker and friend April and she helped validate why I couldn't stop thinking about it. She reminded me of what an important person David was in my life—regardless of what happened, he was a good friend who I consistently spent time with, and who knew a lot about me, my life, and my viewpoints. She told me to listen to my gut to figure out how I felt deep down and what I wanted to do about it.

Listen to my gut—easier said than done. I hate when people tell me that because I never hear my f-ing gut.

Needing a distraction from the situation, I pulled up Instagram. And wouldn't ya know the first picture in my feed was a post by Sara of her and David—complete with the caption, "Our love is fun."

I felt sick to my stomach. *Seriously? This is what she has to post today of all days?* I couldn't believe it.

And then I think my gut chimed in—*Talk to him.*

I pulled up a text and without giving myself time to question it, I texted him that it didn't feel right to act like nothing had happened; that our friendship was too important to me to put it in jeopardy; and that I wanted to talk about what happened. As soon as I sent it, I started freaking out. *Talk to him? What are you even going to say? "You're welcome for stopping us from banging"?*

It was too late. The text was sent. And David responded a couple of minutes later—"I agree."

I left work early—I was mentally checked out with one foot out the door anyway—and on my drive home I tried to think about what I was going to say. Sometimes I plan out entire conversations in my head—what I will start out with, different responses to different reactions, etc. It was hard to do that in this scenario because I still didn't know what I wanted to accomplish with this conversation. I just knew I had to have it, and I hoped it would bring some clarity for me. Sober clarity, this time... just to clarify.

I texted him when I got home and he came over. I couldn't deny my nerves—my heart was pounding and my hands were shaking. I was relieved when I saw the same shake in his hands when he arrived. There was pretty much no small talk. He sat down on the couch... right where the first kiss had happened... and I took a deep breath and just went for it. I started off the conversation by reiterating what I said in my text—"I really care about our relationship and I can't just act like nothing happened. So I thought the adult thing to do would be to talk about what happened...

so, what *did* happen?"

I decided to leave it open-ended to see where he took the conversation. Considering my head was all over the place, I chose reaction over action.

I'll admit I wasn't expecting the explanation I got, although I probably should have been because it was pretty typical—he told me he thought a lot about it over the weekend, so much so that he could barely eat from feeling so guilty. He said he'd never done anything like that before and that if anything more had happened, he wouldn't have been able to live with himself. (So I guess "You're welcome for me stopping us from banging" would have been an appropriate thing to say after all.) And then came the kicker... he said he realized he really did love Sara... and wanted a future with her... blah... blah... blah. And in that moment, I could feel my guard shoot back up and I closed any door to possibility.

"That's good," I said, walls back up, unwilling to show any signs of vulnerability. I asked him if he remembered everything that had been said that night and he replied that he did not. I chose not to tell him that he told me he thought he loved me. I chose not to bring up his comments early in the night about feeling stuck in his relationship; or joking about how, if she cheated on him, that could be his "out." I chose not to go there because none of that mattered. What mattered was what he was saying in that moment, and he was saying he loved her. Who was I to question that? If his words weren't true to his feelings, that was his problem. Not mine.

We talked a little bit more, agreed to not be awkward, and hugged goodbye.

After he left, I still didn't know how I felt. Part of me felt relieved. Part of me felt rejected. Mostly I was confused. How could he have all these questions about their relationship yet choose to stay? And furthermore, how could he say all these things about his feelings for me yet choose to discount them? I didn't know the answers but I definitely knew what I *wasn't* feeling—and that was surprised. Not at all. Because I'd been there before.

JOURNAL ENTRY: jaded, *part 2*

MARCH 2017

So yea, that happened. And that's where I got the idea to give up men for Lent. I'd like to say I had this profound realization that I need space to figure out who I really am, yada, yada, yada. Nope. Honestly, I just need a break from getting my hopes up and from clinging to thoughts like *maybe this one is the one.* It's become this unhealthy pattern—this annoying cycle—that I don't know how to break.

Example: This past January, I was up in Washington D.C. visiting my sister for a girls' weekend with two of our cousins. A classmate of mine from my MBA program was living there and met us out. He's sweet and attractive and I always had a fun flirtation with him, but I never felt any real feelings for him. But that night the attention was much needed, and I got drunk and went home with him... on a family girls' weekend! Who does that? Then for probably a week or two (or maybe even three) after that weekend, guess what I would catch myself doing? Thinking about how maybe I would go visit him and it would spark this great relationship that I never saw coming and I would move to D.C. and we would live happily ever after. (sigh)

Another example: The other week, I got a text from a guy I dated for like a minute last year. Great guy. But no real connection. The text was one of those not-so-obvious-but-still-obvious ploys to see me, joking around about me owing him dinner. And where did my mind go? *Maybe I didn't give him enough of a chance.* (double sigh)

I feel like I've lost control of my life—like I go where I'm wanted, not where I want to go. This is my attempt to gain some of the control back. To hopefully figure out how I—me, myself, and I only—can make myself happy.

Why Lent? Well, even though I'm by no means religious, I was raised Catholic and have always liked the concept of giving up something for Lent. I like the challenge of it. This year I'm really challenging myself by giving up several things I have a love/hate relationship with:

Sweets—I have a serious sweet tooth so having a legit reason to pass on dessert helps me break my sugar addiction.

Social Media—I feel like it just makes me sad sometimes. Or annoyed. I don't want to see pics of happy couples when I'm in bed alone. And I certainly don't want to see seemingly happy pics with overly loving captions of couples who I know aren't actually happy.

Hard liquor—I love me some vodka. But I don't love not clearly remembering nights out. I rarely drink to the point of blackout anymore, but I still sometimes wake up and have that icky feeling as I relive conversations and wish I hadn't said certain things. Or done certain things... like make-out with a good friend. (ugh) Eliminating hard liquor should slow the rate at which I get buzzed, hopefully giving me the chance to decide I've had enough for the night.

Men—How is this going to work exactly? Well...

Rule #1 is that I will not socially reach out to any men in any way. There always seem to be a couple of guys "in the wings" who I can reach out to when I'm feeling lonely. Usually they're out of town so it's not about hanging out with someone—or hooking up with someone. It's more about having someone to chat with… anyone who goes from being in a relationship to being single knows that feeling of suddenly seeing a drastic decrease in text messages. As pathetic as it sounds, it's a tough change.

Rule #2 is that if one of these "wing men"—or even just a guy friend—reaches out to me, I will either not respond or just be honest that I've given up men for Lent and to contact me after Easter. I'm leaning towards the latter—I hate being ignored so I don't want to ignore anyone. Same strategy if a new guy asks me out. That "hard to get" thing seems to work well in the movies.

Exceptions to the rule? Family (obviously), Steve (my personal trainer), and I'm still going to run with David's running group. I really enjoy it and have become friends with several of the regulars. But I won't go out for dinner/drinks afterwards with them, and I'm going to tell David there'll be no more extracurricular chatting for the time being.

I'm hoping that if I reject men first and don't even give them the chance to reject me, I'll get a much-needed break from the disappointment and heartache that have plagued me ever since I started dating.

JOURNAL ENTRY: I've fallen and I can't get up

MARCH 2017

My favorite part of the movie *How to Be Single* is the explanation of "dicksand." An obvious play on quicksand, dicksand is basically the phenomenon of when a girl forgets who she is and gets sucked into the world of the guy she's seeing. After I watched that movie, I texted three of my best friends from my years of living in South Florida (Amber, Taylor, and Charlotte), and said, "That's me. I fall into their dicksand."

My relationships used to be just as the movie explains it. When I was in my 20s and I was dating someone, the dicksand would swallow me whole. I lost myself in them and their life. My schedule always revolved around their schedule. We only did things they wanted to do. I would seek permission to do things with my friends, and I would constantly worry if they were mad at me. If I could remember all the times I apologized for something I shouldn't have apologized for, I'm sure it would make me sick.

It was little things too - I bought a Hispanic cookbook and tried to master *arroz con pollo* just like my boyfriend Arlo liked it. For my boyfriend Charlie, I started drinking dirty martinis and I bought a gun because he liked to go to the gun range. It's like the movie *Runaway Bride*, where she always orders her eggs how her boyfriend likes his. I've never been that extreme, but it's the same concept.

Now, some of it ended up being positive, as I was exposed to new things... some of which I liked. For example, I learned I love plantains, I still drink dirty martinis, and it turns out that I'm a pretty good shot. Silver linings, I guess.

When those relationships ended, my friends were quick to point out that I had lost myself in them. And for the most part, I knew they were right. I put so much energy into convincing myself that I was the girl each of those guys expected me to be and wanted me to be. It's like I was obsessed with making it work no matter what the cost was. (sigh)

I've realized I pour everything into my relationships

and leave nothing for myself. I always thought it was a good trait of mine—that it meant I was all-in, that I really cared. But now I realize the catch-22—when you lose yourself for a man, you lose the parts of you that attracted the man to begin with, the parts of you that connected with him. How can love survive—or even be real—when one party isn't whole? When one person has been consumed by the other? When one person is drowning?

Recently, the dicksand has been more shallow in my life, but it's still there—whenever a new guy enters the picture in any capacity, I allow my mind to go down the road of our potential life together instead of taking the time to think about if he is what I want. I focus solely on being wanted instead of what I want. I start to think too much about what I say or how I act instead of just being me. I over analyze how to respond to a text, thinking through different options, trying to figure out how to get the response I want. I realized this a while ago but even after realizing it, I continued to catch myself doing it. Hence giving up men for Lent... I'm trying to keep a safe distance from any/all dicksand. Hopefully I can regain my footing on solid ground.

JOURNAL ENTRY: making an *ass* out of *u* and *me*, *part 1*

MARCH 2017

Today, my younger brother, Alex, and his wife, Kimberly, found out they're pregnant. I'm crying. Just like I cried when I found out they were engaged. I hate how cliché it is—the older sister upset that her younger brother gets married and has kids before her.

People never understand. They tell me "you're beautiful," "you're smart," "you're a catch," "you'll meet someone." But what everyone seems to forget is that my love life so far has mostly been filled with disappointment and heartbreak. Am I supposed to just forget all that and trust that their compliments and predictions for my life? If I'm such a catch, why has no one caught me? If I'm so smart, why do I keep getting into situations that end up hurting me?

My poor mother. We were on the phone earlier

talking about Alex and Kimberly being pregnant, and she picked up on something in my voice and asked, "Are you okay?" How does she always know I'm upset before even I do? It's crazy how the ones you're closest to always bring out the emotions you try to bury the deepest. I say "my poor mother" because I punish her for that. I avoid talking to her and build my emotional walls just a little bit taller, all the while putting on a smile, meeting her for lunch, texting constantly, and saying I'm fine. I avoid *really* talking to her. She knows I'm not fine and she wants desperately to access my thoughts and my heart and to make everything okay. Instead of letting her in, I answer like always that "I'm fine"—and quickly get off the phone so I can let the tears that have welled up start to fall.

Lately I feel like a stranger in my family. Like they don't know who I really am and they're all heading down a different path than me. Everyone has followed the "get married and have babies" protocol and I somehow missed that step. Our paths have always been seemingly parallel but that missed step has caused a slight veer and now we're starting to get further and further apart. It's like I've gone rogue.

And the ironic part of all of it is that everyone always assumed I would get married young. I always had boyfriends growing up and then I fell in love for the first time - like, *really* fell in love—when I was 16 years old. My family loved him too—he was constantly at our house, hanging out or having dinner with us. He even came on a family vacation with us. He was like family—like I had the first go at bringing an outsider into the inner circle and they completely accepted him. I bet they even assumed that we would end up together. Well, maybe not assumed, given they likely knew the odds of teenage love lasting forever weren't in our favor. But I'm sure they thought it was at least in the realm of possibility. I, on the other hand, absolutely assumed we would end up together. That "get married and have babies" box was preemptively checked in my mind.

I assumed wrong.

LOOKING BACK: *the one* that got away

2001-2013

AGE: 16-28

Highschool 2001

My first love's name was Lloyd. He was also only 16 years old when we fell in love. I've since realized there are pros and cons to falling in love that young:

Pros: You learn and experience the depth and scope of your feelings early in your life. Cons: You learn and experience the depth and scope of your feelings early in your life.

Love is an intense emotion on its own and the youth factor just further complicates it. I'm not sure I was mature enough to handle all my feelings. Let me rephrase that—I *know* I wasn't mature enough to handle all my feelings. And for everyone who also fell in love when their age ended in *teen*, you know exactly what I'm talking about.

I loved Lloyd so much. I lost my virginity to him and in many ways, I lost my mind. It was the first time— but would not be the last time—I put a guy before my family, before my friendships, and even before myself. He and our relationship became my world. When we fought, I was devastated. When we weren't fighting, I was blissfully in love, daydreaming about our future life together. First love becomes forever love—who doesn't love that story?

(Ironically, I'm watching a young, high school-aged couple fight as I write this. I'm sitting outside at a coffee shop and they're at the table next to me. They're arguing over whether or not she called him stupid. Every look and movement is filled with exasperated emotion. She's blankly staring in the other direction, clearly sending the message that she's pissed. She doesn't get the attention from him she wants, so not even a minute later, she reaches out to touch his leg. They start whispering about something, and the affection and loving looks resume. I can't help but laugh to myself because I've *so* been there.)

Despite my "crazy girlfriend" tendencies in my

young love relationship with Lloyd, I was smart enough not to follow him to college. He decided to go to the University of Georgia and I went to FSU, where my father went and where my older sister was. Lloyd and I were going to do the dreaded long-distance relationship thing. And to make it even more challenging, we both went the Greek life route which pretty much meant one thing—any excuse to party.

College 2002 - 2006

Lloyd and I survived freshman year with frequent trips to see each other or meet in Jacksonville. But it was not without its fair share of jealousy-infused worrying, control-issue arguments, and immature, moody conversations where someone was constantly asking the other, "What's wrong?"

The summer after freshman year, we made what we thought was a mature decision—we decided to break up before starting our sophomore year. We agreed that being in a long-distance relationship in college didn't make sense and that we should both go all-in and get the most out of our years at school since we could never go back. Amazingly, I was at the forefront of this decision. I guess I recognized there were many nights during that first year where I opted not to go out with my friends for fear that he would be upset. Or maybe I was tired of lectures from my mother and sister about how I shouldn't let my relationship ruin my college experience… which was apparently supposed to include going out partying all the time. Or maybe it was the desire to not have to deal with calling him when I got home, worrying that he would be mad, and then reassuring him that I wasn't interested in any of the guys I met.

He was so upset when we said goodbye at the end of that summer. I remember standing with him in my parents' driveway, watching the tears roll down his face, and thinking I should feel more upset than I was. I *was* sad, of course, but mostly I was excited to be free. Not free from him, but free from the guilt and worry and drama that existed in our long-distance relationship; and free from all the strong opinions from the other relationships in my life.

I didn't want to meet other guys. I just didn't want to worry about what anyone else thought anymore.

In my mind, it wasn't that big of a deal in the bigger picture because we would get back together either later in college or after college, and still live out the life together that I had planned on. So I started sophomore year ready to party. And man did I! I was living in the sorority house in the same room as three of my best friends, with another best friend in the room next door. We went out all the time— Monday night was Painted Lady, Tuesday was nickel beer night at Potbelly's, Wednesday was for sorority/ fraternity Socials (themed parties), Thursday was Power Hour at Late Night Library, Friday was happy hour at Potbelly's, Saturday was game day during football season, and on Sunday we would recover. We had a blast.

I quickly built a reputation for being someone who was always down to go out and stay out. And I was proud of that. I never had the sexiest or trendiest outfit and I was never the prettiest girl in the room, but I was happy being the girl who was smart, fun, and witty. I was the girl who could keep up. I nestled into my label as a "party girl"—a label I would enjoy for many years to come.

During my drunken nights out and exhausted days in class, I often thought of Lloyd and missed him. I wondered if he was having as much fun as I was. But I partied on, never really letting the thoughts of him last too long.

When I was home for Christmas break of sophomore

year, surrounded by memories of him at every turn, I decided to mail him a Christmas present... a true act of first love dramatic flair. I don't think we had spoken since we said goodbye at the end of summer. I believe we agreed not to, knowing talking would make the decision to not be together more difficult. Thinking back on it, that too might have been my idea because I didn't want to feel like I was being held back in any way. And I guess I knew I didn't have the strength not to care if he was upset that I was going out. The Christmas present prompted a phone call, which resulted in a lunch, which turned into a couple more hang-outs, and before I knew it, we were heading back to school. We continued to communicate and even took turns visiting each other a couple of times. Things were going well...

...until I dropped the bomb on him that I had slept with someone else during the first term when we hadn't been talking.

I hadn't technically done anything wrong because we weren't together, but I felt like he needed to know... because I thought I would want to know. My friends begged me not to tell him, but I remember feeling like I *had* to.

So I did.

And it didn't go well.

He was both furious and devastated. I became the bad guy and I allowed myself to be the bad guy. I could have argued that I did nothing wrong. I could have argued that he should forgive me as quickly as I forgave him for sleeping with someone else in a drunken stupor during the summer session before our freshmen year. (Because yea, that happened. And I forgave him.) But I don't think I even brought any of that up. Probably because I wasn't ready to be back in a place where I had ties to someone who could affect how I lived my life. Accepting my role as the bad guy allowed me to keep my freedom without it being my decision to end the situation, which was starting to feel all too much like a long-distance relationship again.

Apparently I knew that I still didn't have the strength to just do what I wanted to do without caring about someone else's reaction... even if that reaction was unfounded.

Sophomore year ended in a continued drunken blur of nights out and foggy next days. My group of friends became extremely close and I was happy. I felt like I knew who I was at school—I was independent and confident in my party-girl role. But when I went home, the memories from my relationship with Lloyd and the ghosts of the more insecure version of myself in that relationship haunted me—looking out the window, anxiously waiting for him to come over; hiding in a different room, crying from a stupid argument; playing songs and asking him to listen to the lyrics. Those ghosts made me sad... and sick to my stomach. I decided to take summer classes that year so I could stay in Tallahassee.

Fast forward to Fall and the football season of my junior year. There was a big football game in Tallahassee and through mutual friends, I knew Lloyd was in town for it. Despite it being a big school, I felt super-anxious about possibly running into him. So I did what any other 21-year-old avoiding her feelings would do—I drank. I got so drunk at the tailgate that I didn't even make it to the game. I woke up on the couch at the sorority house just in time to see my team lose. I made no effort to muster the energy to go out to the bars and instead ordered pizza with everyone else who had a little too much fun too early.

The next day my little sister in the sorority, who was also from Jacksonville, told me she saw Lloyd out after the game at Potbelly's. I wasn't surprised— that was the most popular bar. Her facial expression changed to sadness as she paused before adding, "He was with someone."

Now that did surprise me. It shouldn't have—it had been a while since we'd been together and it was college. People date a lot in college. But it was Lloyd. He was my first love. I still loved him. In my mind, we still belonged together. He was mine. In that moment I understood his reaction to my "someone else" news.

My sorority sister went on to tell me how the girl was wearing these weird, big earrings and other trivial insults in an attempt to lessen the blow. But I still burst into tears.

The thought of him with someone else crushed me. But for me, it wasn't so much the physical part of things. What really tore at my heart was the question *what if it's a serious relationship?* Just like he couldn't handle me giving my body to someone else, I couldn't handle him giving his heart to someone else.

Not long after that, Facebook arrived on the internet. The first time someone showed it to me, I asked them to search to see if he was on it—he was. So I refused to join. Throughout junior year, my friends would tell me about things they saw on his Facebook page—i.e. pictures of him with the mystery girl—but I never allowed myself to look. I visited home several times but never ran into him, and neither of us reached out to the other. I continued to live a very social life with my friends while somehow managing good grades and working towards a double major. I took summer classes again that year—I'm not sure I saw or spoke to Lloyd at all my junior year.

Senior year started at a slower pace than my sophomore and junior years. Two years of frequenting the same bars and seeing the same people had started to wear on me. I still went out a lot, but it had definitely lost a bit of its luster. When I was home over Christmas break that year, I went out drinking one night with my sister. We'd been at a big neighborhood Christmas party all day and decided to continue the fun at a local hole-in-the-wall bar in a shopping center not far from my parents' house. We walked in, and *BAM*—there was Lloyd.

Talk about not expecting to see someone—we were at a tiny bar on my parents' side of town. His parents lived twenty minutes away. And who even knew about that little bar?

I was shocked. I was drunk. I didn't have time to think because he was literally right in front of me.

I briefly said hello to him. I was cordial while my sister stood behind me, I'm sure giving him the death stare. I don't remember what we talked about, but I know it wasn't for long so I assume it was the basic, "How are you? How's the family? How's school?" bullshit. My sister and I then posted up at the bar. She looked at me worried and asked, "Are you okay?"

"Yep," I said blankly, not wanting to even try to decipher my feelings. "Shots?"

Later that night, when we got back to my parents' house, we woke my mother up to tell her that we ran into him. We talked to her for a bit downstairs in the kitchen while drunk eating before retreating to our childhood bedrooms to pass out. When I got back to my room, I checked my old-school Nokia flip phone. I stood there in shock—I had two missed calls from him. I panicked for a minute, and then called him back.

Now remember, I took the "drink until you don't feel feelings anymore" strategy after seeing him, so not surprisingly I couldn't remember much of our conversation the next day. There were only a couple of key things I remembered—that he said he never stopped loving me even though he had been with his girlfriend (Danielle) for a while; that one night in his sleep he said, "I love you, Kacie," and she got really upset (understandably so); that her mom was dying of cancer; and that he cared about her and didn't want to hurt her.

I tried so hard to remember the rest of our conversation. What did I say back to all of that? How did we leave things? I had no idea.

I left it all alone and headed back to Tallahassee to finish college.

A couple of weeks before graduation, out of nowhere, he called me. It was on a random weeknight and it was early, so I'm pretty sure it wasn't a drunk dial. He told me that he and Danielle had broken up. We talked for a while and decided to see each other. My best friend Taylor was dating someone in law school at UGA so it was no trouble convincing her to go visit with me.

Seeing him this time was different. He was more arrogant than he used to be... like the popped collar fraternity life had gotten to him. I felt different too... like I reverted back to a less self-assured, smaller version of myself. Despite not feeling the same connection, I stayed with him that night. I think I couldn't let go of how I used to feel about him and all the years of emotions surrounding our relationship. In my imagination, it would be this movie-like reunion full of passion. In reality, it was two kids who had lost their virginity to each other years before and hadn't made a ton of progress since.

We said goodbye the next day with no talk of what, if anything, the future was for us. What was the point? He was staying in Georgia after graduation to start law school, and I was moving south, having accepted a job with a public relations firm in Ft. Lauderdale.

Summer 2006

A couple of weeks after graduation, I permanently moved out of my parents' house, left my hometown, and moved into my new apartment, in a new city, to start my first job. It was time to be an adult.

It was a difficult adjustment for me. Sometimes I would cry about it on the phone with friends who were lucky enough to still be in Tallahassee for grad school. Other times I would laugh about it, joking with my dad about my realization that my alarm clock was never going to stop going off. Lloyd and I communicated a little, but not much. Texting had become more popular and we texted here and there at first, but eventually even that faded into zero communication. He was one of those people lucky enough to still be in a college town for grad school, so his alarm probably didn't have to go off every day.

Fall 2006

I found out through some serious Myspace stalking one night—yes, Myspace, because I was still refusing to join Facebook, thinking it was just a fad—that him and Danielle were back together. I burst into tears. I guess she decided to also pursue a graduate degree at UGA. Well played, Danielle, well played.

I was hurt, but mostly I was confused. I never got any explanation. He told me he still loved me and didn't really want to be with Danielle, then broken up with her and reached out to me, then disappeared, and then got back together with her? (See what I mean about having been in the David situation before?) I understand that relationships are complicated, but how could he tell me he loved me and not her, and then choose to go back to her instead of choosing me? I just didn't understand. Maybe I should have been more aggressive in keeping the communication going. And maybe my belief that men should pursue women (not the other way around) had really just left the door open for Danielle to swoop back in.

Fall 2007

I knew it was over between Lloyd and I—it had been years since we'd really been together and now our lives were on completely separate paths. But I still felt like there were so many things left unsaid. I needed closure. One night I had a dream about him—one of those dreams that feels so real you wake up confused about what day or year it is. I woke up in the middle of the night after the dream and couldn't go back to sleep... so I wrote him a letter.

I acknowledged that when we reconnected towards the end of college, we were both in weird places in our lives, trying to navigate the transition from college life to adult life, or college life to grad school life in his case. I confessed that I was upset when I found out he was back together with Danielle; that I felt betrayed—like all the things he said to me about his feelings had been a lie. And how, for the longest time, I just wanted to know why—why he called me when they broke up, why he told me he never stopped caring about me, and of course why he disappeared.

I confessed that I thought I was too young to really handle my feelings for him when we were together— that there were many situations I wished I could go back in time and change; many conversations I should have handled differently; and many arguments that didn't need to be so dramatic. But I also recognized how much him and our relationship had taught me about life.

I told him that I didn't want or need a response to the letter—that it was just my way of finally really saying goodbye. I said I had no bad feelings towards him or the way anything had gone down, and that I just wanted him to be happy. I recognized that our lives were on different paths, and while we would likely never be friends, I felt grateful for the role he played in my life.

...Our relationship and the times we had together will forever be a part of me and I gladly carry those memories with me always.

Having no clue where he lived in Georgia, I mailed it to his parents' house asking them to get it to him. Again with the first love dramatic flair.

I did not get a response to the letter. And while I

explicitly said I didn't want or need a response, I still remember the feeling of disappointment as the days went by and I didn't get one.

I think 2008... maybe 2009

I was doing some casual Facebook stalking—yes, I finally realized it wasn't a fad and joined—and I learned Lloyd and Danielle got engaged through a photo she posted.

As I looked at the picture, I surprisingly didn't burst into tears this time. I remember feeling mostly sad but slightly happy for him, with a small side of disappointment. She was getting the life I had pictured with him... the life that he and I used to talk about—a life together. I don't think I still loved him at that point, but it was difficult accepting the idea that it really was over, and that there would be no next chapter for us. I'd be lying if I said there hadn't been a part of me that still wondered (or maybe even hoped) that they would break up and we would reconnect. That whole "if you truly love someone, let them go and see if they come back to you" thing. I had let him go, but deep down I always wanted him to come back. And now I knew he never would.

Probably 2011

He randomly popped into my universe. He was
working as a lawyer and had a meeting with someone
in the law firm where my dad worked so he stopped
by my dad's office to say hello. After my dad told
me about it, I decided to Facebook friend request
him and included a message saying my dad told me
they saw each other, and I figured enough time had
passed that we could at least be Facebook friends.
He accepted and responded with something agreeing
and asking how I was doing. There wasn't much back
and forth after that.

Probably 2013

I was in bed scrolling through Facebook and saw
that they were pregnant. I burst into tears. And
immediately de-friended him. The tears weren't so
much because they were pregnant... I knew that day
would come after they got married. It was more the
glaringly obvious difference between where our lives
were... there he was living the life I had planned
with him but with someone else, and there I was
crying about it alone in bed. In that moment, there

was no avoiding the flaws in my own life. I was in a bad relationship situation with marriage and babies nowhere in my near future—because my current boyfriend was already married with babies.

Lloyd was doing everything we were supposed to be doing—dominating the "married with babies" protocol. I felt like he was winning in the game of life… and I hadn't even gotten off the bench.

JOURNAL ENTRY: making an *ass* out of *u* and *me, part 2*

MARCH 2017

I think my family struggled to get over Lloyd almost as much as I did—hating giving up on the idea that we would never have another shot. Of course it didn't help that all the relationships I got into after Lloyd weren't exactly the greatest of situations. It was like I went from Captain America to the Island of Misfit Men.

Now I just feel like my family constantly feels sorry for me. Like when they ask about my dating life, behind their voices is this hint of sadness. An assumption that I must be unhappy and lonely. My sister-in-law has tried to hook me up with everyone from random guys at the bar, to an Uber driver, to the manager of a resort we often vacation at. And my mother probably gets more excited than I do when I start dating someone new. She's definitely also thinking *maybe this one is the one*—and watching her go through the *hopes up then let down* is maybe worse than actually experiencing it.

Even my dad's in on it. One time my parents came and met up with me and some friends to watch a basketball game at a bar. The group included several people I didn't know, most of whom were guys. I caught my dad looking at some of the guys while leaning over and whispering to my mom. I knew what he was saying. I asked my mom about it later and I was right—

"These guys seem nice. Why doesn't she date one of them?"

I know it comes from a good place. I know they just want me to be happy... but that adopts the assumption that I'm unhappy. That my current life is wrong in some way. And while yes, I've just realized that that assumption is correct, and I am in fact unhappy, that's not the point. I guess the point is that I want to be the only one who can determine if I'm unhappy... and more importantly, *why* I'm unhappy.

I don't know—maybe I'm just embarrassed to still be single at this point in my life. But maybe it's deeper than that... maybe it's the assumption that I need to be married to be happy that doesn't sit right with me.

Maybe what looks like going rogue to them is right for me.

JOURNAL ENTRY: the day YouTube changed my life

MARCH 2017

Today I went to the gym after work. When you give up men and liquor, there isn't much else to do on a Friday evening. Plus, after the marathon, I set a goal to reach 20% body fat before I go on a cruise with my MBA friends in mid-April.

I chose the gym over the running group even though the running group always goes for tacos after the run on Fridays… and I love tacos. I just didn't feel like seeing David. Earlier this week, I told him I was giving up men for Lent and he got really upset. He blamed himself. I tried to explain that it wasn't his fault—he was just the straw that broke the camel's back. Later that night I texted him:

I probably shouldn't have told you that and I'm sorry for doing so. My intention was not to make you feel bad in any way. I think you think you hurt me - you didn't. Don't worry, I don't think we are meant to be anything more than really great friends, and if you remembered everything that was said on Friday, you would remember my thought process on that because I was very honest. The pattern I need to find a way to break is men telling me things - whether I want to hear them or not - that they don't actually mean or just won't actually face. You don't know the details of my relationship history, but it happens all the time and I can't take it anymore. And in that respect, you do have some shit you need to work out - because you said a lot of things on Friday that aren't consistent with your sober line of thinking, or you just haven't consciously faced those thoughts yet. Either way, I'll always be your friend, I want nothing but happiness for you, and I'm here to listen... just after I cleanse all this negative energy.

I imagine that will be the last time either of us references what happened between us. There's nothing more to say.

The gym was not crowded and about halfway through my workout, everyone had left except my personal trainer, Steve, and me. With no one else in the gym, no clients to train, and me busy with a workout he had written for me, Steve decided to do his own workout for the day. I know from walking in on him training early in the mornings that he likes to listen to motivational speeches when he works out. They aren't what you're probably imagining—they're snippets of motivational messages from all kinds of different successful people (athletes, celebrities, motivational speakers, etc.) compiled together with music in the background. I wasn't really feeling the music that was on in the gym so I told him I was okay with him putting on his motivational messages while we worked out. He did.

I wasn't paying a lot of attention to what the motivational people were saying at first... I went about my business, rowing for a minute and then walking back to the incline ab bench to do sit-ups. Then, before I knew it, I caught myself sitting on the rowing machine not rowing, just listening. Over the speakers of the gym, a voice I didn't recognize— some famous or successful person I don't know— was asking me, "Do you ever just feel off and can't explain why?"

Yes.

"Do you ever feel unhappy or unfulfilled in life, but don't know the reason?"

Yes.

I never really thought I felt unfulfilled in life—how

could I? I have a great life. But as I sat motionless on the rower, mouth probably open, brow furrowed, there was no escaping my answer. *Yes, I feel unfulfilled and don't know the reason.*

Then the voice abruptly cut off and was replaced by Pitbull yelling "Timber!" I looked up and saw that Steve had changed it back to music because other people had come into the gym.

Damnit. I wanted to hear what it said next.

I went back to my workout, wishing I could hear what that motivational person was going to say next and feeling a little uneasy at having just admitted to myself that I felt unfulfilled. Before I left the gym, I asked Steve where he gets the motivational stuff. I wanted to keep listening. I wanted to know what that voice was going to say next—why I feel off or what to do about it. He told me to search 'Fearless Motivation' on YouTube.

When I got home, I immediately turned on my TV, went to the YouTube app on my Roku (for maybe the first time ever), searched for 'Fearless Motivation', and played the first video that came up.

I listened as I did things around the house—started laundry, cleaned up a bit, made dinner. Surprisingly,

I found myself enjoying the videos. I say 'surprisingly' because historically, I'm not someone who's at all into motivational speakers or self-help in any way. My best friend from South Florida, Amber, has always been into that stuff and tried to get me to watch *The Secret* many years ago. I made her turn it off after about two minutes, laughing and telling her it was ridiculous. I like clever or thought-provoking quotes and that's about it.

But I was truly enjoying these little snippets of people talking. I got my dinner together and sat down on the couch to keep watching. "Watching" is a stretch because it wasn't a video at all—the image on the screen was a static picture of a very in-shape, shirtless, sweaty man with his mouth open like he was yelling. So I was really just sitting on the couch, dinner plate in hand, looking at an unchanging picture (an odd sight, I'm sure). And then the video asked a question that punched me in the gut—

"What is your purpose?"

I don't know.

It went on. "What drives you?"

I don't know.

The torture continued. "Why do you get out of bed in the morning? Why are you here?"

I don't know. I don't know!

I sat there stunned, thinking *how do I not know what my purpose is? I'm almost thirty-three years old and I've literally never thought about this. And no one has ever asked me. How is that possible? Why am I here?*

I was very disturbed and a little annoyed that I didn't know the answers to these questions. And worse— that I never even thought about them.

JOURNAL ENTRY: a purposeful walk

MARCH 2017

Today I woke up determined to figure it out. I got up early and walked to the beach to watch the sunrise. I brought my phone and my earbuds and put those YouTube videos back on, allowing them to continuously play. I went for a long walk, just listening and thinking, trying to figure out my purpose in life. I tried to think about what really makes me happy, what brings me fulfillment, and what I really want to do. I thought back as far as I could and just let whatever memories that came to mind surface...

My mind first jumped back to a memory when I was very young. No idea how old or where I was, but I remember my uncle laughing at something I said and telling me I was going to grow up to be a comedian. And I remember that comment made me very happy. That memory sticks with me to this day and I've never known why. Perhaps it's because I do love making people laugh. I've always been quick witted—it's easily one of my favorite traits about myself.

Random memory. Interesting clue. I filed it away and kept thinking...

I flashed back to another memory when I was a little bit older, probably around twelve. It was Thanksgiving. Our Thanksgiving Day traditions involved the men of the family sitting in one room around a big TV watching football, and the women in the living room chatting. I was the youngest, with my sister two years older than me and then the closest-aged cousin seven years older than her. I remember getting into a conversation with my older cousin Beth about her friend's relationship that wasn't going well, and how Beth didn't know what to do to help her friend. I can't recall the specifics, but I spent a long time talking it through with her, analyzing it and giving my advice. Who was I to be giving advice about an adult relationship? I was a kid! The extent of my relationships at that time had been holding hands during a movie. But after the conversation, Beth looked at me and sincerely thanked me, saying I gave really good advice, especially for someone my age. In that moment, I remember really loving the feeling of what I was too young to understand then but is clear to me now—I enjoy analyzing someone else's situation or life and providing insight to (hopefully) help them.

Another random memory that's still with me.

(As I type this, I can't help but think of the movie *Inside Out* and how these memories are like the brightly colored balls—the core memories in my life that helped shape who I am.)

(Wow, that actually really makes sense...)

More brightly-colored ball memories started to pop up in my mind. I thought about how I wanted to be a child psychologist when I first went to college. Again—analyzing a life and helping someone navigate through it.

I recalled how after a couple years out of college, I wasn't happy in my Corporate America job and considered joining the Peace Corps. Not sure what that one's telling me—a desire to help? To make a difference? Interest in travel?

I thought about how several years ago, when I really got into running half-marathons, I encouraged several people to run their first half-marathon and how happy I was when they did it. Motivating people?

As I sifted through all these memories and things I enjoy, a theme started to surface—helping people. But it wasn't limited to people who necessarily needed help—like with the half-marathon people, it wasn't that they had something wrong and needed help. They were going about life just fine. But I wanted them to see they were capable of something they originally thought they couldn't do or were afraid to do. I wanted to show them they were capable of more than they thought they were.

As I pieced these puzzle pieces together—laughter, navigating life, encouraging people to accomplish things they thought they couldn't—I realized what the puzzle said: I want to make other people's lives better. Again, *better* isn't assuming there's anything wrong with their lives, but things can always be better. I like to inspire people to do more; to become a better version of themselves.

Is "make other people's lives better" my purpose? I repeated it a couple times in my head as I walked. It felt good, but something was off... so I kept thinking. *What am I missing?*

And then it hit me. *What about me?* I like all those things too. I love to laugh. I analyze my own life (clearly). I like to do things I originally thought I couldn't (ahem, MBA; ahem, marathon). I like to better myself. It's not just other people's lives I want to make better—it's my life, too. There's nothing wrong with my life on paper, but clearly there is something off or I wouldn't feel as disconnected as I do. Maybe it's because I'm meant to do more. If I use the same logic on myself that I do with other people, then maybe I'm capable of more than I've been thinking I am.

It's like I've just been coasting through life but not *really* thinking about it or questioning it. I've just been consumed with my love life and my social life... but there has to be more than that. I don't even know what that "more" looks like, but I feel deep inside me that it exists... and I have to figure it out. That's probably why I feel like I don't have control of my life... maybe I'm not really living *my* life. I've been bouncing from boyfriend to boyfriend, from bar to bar, not questioning if there's another direction I could be heading in.

Make life better. That's it. I just knew it. I want to make life better. Maybe that's my greater purpose in life or maybe it's just what I need to do right now... I don't know... but I know something about it feels very right.

I repeated that phrase in my head and smiled. It was

like a huge sigh of relief in my heart. I had a new way to look at life and make decisions—something either makes life better or it doesn't. It's that simple. Now everything can finally make sense. Some clear direction. No more aimlessly bouncing around.

And no more coasting either. I'm going to be intentional about it.

As I ended my walk, I started to think about how I've typically spent my time and what does or doesn't align with making life better:

I run and work out—yep, that's good.

I go to work—that's a necessity, but I wonder if there's a way to make this align more?

I eat pretty healthy—good but could be better.

Sometimes I binge watch Netflix—hmmm, there are probably more productive things I can do with my time.

Alcohol-tastic weekends—tough argument that that one makes life better.

Hmmm, how else do I spend my time? That can't be it, can it? *Crap.*

This is not going to be easy but I have to figure it out—there has to be more. I don't want to feel off and not know why. I don't want to feel apathetic about life. I want to change my life. I want to live my purpose. I want to make life better... whatever that looks like. I don't really know what comes next, but I'm going to figure it out. This is my new mission... my next stage.

JOURNAL ENTRY: a walk off track, *part 1*

MARCH 2017

Today I had plans to walk on the beach with my friend and former coworker, April. Since I started my new job, we no longer see each other every day so we've made a point of getting together regularly to catch up.

One thing I love about my friendship with April is that we get real fast. We don't waste time with the bullshit pleasantries of small talk. We get right to the point. That's how we've always been actually—when she first joined our team at my old job, we spent a day together manning a booth at a conference. We started chatting and I asked her what her relationship status was. She's young and attractive and as much as I personally hate being asked that question, I was genuinely curious. She stepped out on an honesty ledge a little—and I'm so happy she did—and told me that she was in a relationship... a same-sex relationship.

"Oh really?" I said. "I would have never guessed that, but that's awesome. Good for you."

She immediately told me her concerns about other people at work knowing and asked that I not say anything to the rest of our team. Jacksonville isn't exactly the most progressive city so I didn't blame her for being reluctant to share this news with people she didn't know well, let alone coworkers. I guess she could immediately tell that I was genuinely accepting of the secret she just shared so she told me a little about her girlfriend and then asked about my love life. I decided to open up a bit too. Without going into specifics on any one relationship, I gave her a brief overview of how I had some bad experiences and was now a little jaded. Since she shared a big secret with me, I decided to reciprocate and told her mine—that I'd been "the other woman."

(I'll get to that story later but I've found that I confess this secret to people when I think they've reached a point of liking me enough that they won't judge me. It's almost like a test. This was the quickest I ever shared that information with someone.)

She didn't judge me for a second and instead shared that she too had been in a relationship with someone who was married... a woman. "So I've been with a married woman—top that," she said in a jokingly almost proud way.

I immediately started laughing and could barely get out, "So have I."

Her face was priceless. "Wait, what???"

"Well,"—I laughed, my face turning bright red I'm sure—"since we are sharing secrets..." I then proceeded to tell her how about a year before, I had a threesome with a married couple. The guy was a friend of mine and it was something he and his wife were into. When I got the invitation, I just thought *why not?* At that time in my life, I figured since I wasn't in a relationship and wasn't having much luck dating, I might as well try to have some unique sexual experiences. YOLO, right?

Ever since that fifteen minutes of airing some of our dirtiest laundry, April and I have never held back with each other. She quickly became one of my closest friends.

As we walked down the beach today, I told her all about the YouTube videos and how disturbed I was that I didn't know my purpose. I told her about my beach walk yesterday and my thought process of trying to figure it out. She was genuinely excited for me and proud of me for reflecting on my life like that. I told her how strange I thought it was that I was just now even thinking about my purpose, and she started inquiring as to why I think that's the case.

"I'm not sure..." I said. "I think maybe I've been too focused on what other people have wanted for my life..."

LOOKING BACK: a choice career

2001-NOW

AGE: 18-32

End of Highschool 2001-2002

I wanted to go out of state for college. My sister was
at Florida State University (where my father had also
gone), but I had it in my head that I wanted to go to
school outside of Florida. For some reason, I wanted
to go to UNC Chapel Hill. I had no connection to
North Carolina and no real reason to want to go
there, but for whatever reason, I did. Mostly, I didn't
want to follow in my sister's footsteps. Not that there
was anything wrong with that—my sister and I have
always been close—but I guess it was a desire to live
my *own* life. A different life than what had seemingly
been laid out for me.

I applied for several schools in the southeast outside of Florida—Clemson, Auburn, Georgia, and NC State. I did apply to one school in-state—FSU—but guess what? I never even applied to UNC Chapel Hill. I remember looking up the requirements and fearing I wouldn't get accepted. It was supposed to be my "stretch school" and I didn't have the courage to apply. So clearly I didn't go there. Apparently you have to apply to a school in order to be accepted. (shrug)

I did get in to all the schools I actually applied for though, and my parents and I went on a road trip to visit all of them. It was a fun weekend—touring the campuses and imagining my life at each of them. It was nerve-wracking and exciting. How was I going to make this huge decision?

A week or so after the trip, I went to lunch with my dad to tell him where I had decided to go. I was very nervous about this conversation. I can remember it pretty clearly—sitting across from him at a booth at a Chili's or Applebee's or something like that—and telling him I wanted to go to Auburn.

Phew! I said it.

Why Auburn? The only reason I can remember is how beautiful it was there. The trees and the rolling hills... it was just so different and serene looking. I remember picturing myself sitting on one of its grassy hills and reading. (In reality, I don't think I spent a single moment sitting on a grassy hill and reading in college.)

My dad didn't react immediately. He took a moment and thought about what he was going to say. I didn't expect what came next.

He calmly and carefully articulated something along the lines of, "It doesn't make sense for you to go out of state when we did Florida Pre-Pay and you have a 100% Bright Futures Scholarship to go to a school in-state. If you wanted to go to a school that was significantly academically better than FSU, it would make sense. But Auburn is no better than FSU academically." He then cut a deal with me—if I stayed in-state for undergrad, he would pay for me to go wherever I wanted for grad school.

I went to FSU.

I can't be upset with him because his logic made perfect sense. I'm really only justified to be upset with myself for not even applying to UNC Chapel Hill. That school *was* significantly academically better than FSU. But regardless, I still could have argued back. I could have told him that, for whatever reason, it was important to me to go out of state; to not follow my older sister. If I had explained that to him, I bet he would have listened. If I had known my dad then like I know him now, I would have known that my happiness matters more to him than any amount of money. But I didn't have the self-awareness to understand why I wanted to go somewhere different for college, let alone to fight for it. So I just went along with what someone else wanted... what someone else expected of me.

Going into college, I planned to major in Psychology, with the goal of becoming a child psychologist. This dream started after a summer job with a local nonprofit that helped underprivileged communities. It provided programs, including a summer camp, for the children of those communities. My mother has been involved in the nonprofit sector of Jacksonville for almost her entire career, and at the time she was the interim executive director for the nonprofit. So the summer after my senior year in high school, I was a camp counselor for the four- and five-year-old children at the summer camp. The relationship that I formed with a couple of the children left a significant imprint on me. There was one in particular—a little boy named JaShawn—who to this day I find myself wondering about, thinking about how his life turned out.

JaShawn was not a good kid by any definition of the word. He got into fights with the other children; he didn't listen to adults; he threw temper tantrums when he didn't get his way. He was stubborn. He was a bully. It was easy to look at him and see the man he would likely become and think trying to change him would be a waste of energy.

But for some reason we connected. Blame my love of a challenge, but I made it a goal to break through to him that summer. I quickly found my first "in"— he wanted to learn how to swim. Each day, all the children spent a couple of hours in the pool. For the most part, my responsibility was to watch them and make sure no one drowned. And the majority of the children would just splash around on the edge of the pool and do their own thing.

But not JaShawn. He wanted to learn how to swim. And he was determined. He would monopolize my time... "Miss Kacie! Miss Kacie! Can I swim to you?"

As soon as I acknowledged him, but before I could even say "yes" or "no," he'd be flailing through the water on his way to me. Now JaShawn was not an affectionate child. He never wanted hugs or to hold hands and would literally pull away if you tried to touch him. But when he swam to me, he had no choice but to hold on to me for dear life because he knew he had to take a break before he could swim back to the wall. I remember those moments of him holding on to my neck, out of breath from the swim over—him knowing that if I pulled away like he always did, he would be in trouble... but I never did. I was there for him every time he wanted to swim to me. And each time I pushed him to go further than he thought he could go, and he did. And in those moments, a trust between us started to form.

JaShawn had another goal in camp. He wanted to win this spaceship computer game they had on a computer in the play room. The game was actually a math game and in order to advance, you had to do basic addition and subtraction. But he didn't see it as that. He just knew there were spaceships involved. He was only five and likely already a little behind in his academic development, so most of the addition and subtraction was over his head. He would call me over, wanting an answer so that he could advance to the next level. I'd push him to figure out how to solve the problem until he reached a boiling point of frustration, and then I would usually give him the answer. But sometimes he did get to the answer all on his own.

On the bus to different field trips throughout the summer, I would always sit next to him. If I didn't, he would likely get in a fight with the kid who did. But also, it gave me an opportunity to try to talk to him without him having anywhere else to go. I would ask a lot of questions and in the beginning, his answers were very short… but over time, he started to talk a little more.

The entire summer was a battle with him. I would try to break through his rough exterior and he would test my patience and push me away. But somehow, I knew I was getting through to him. It wasn't until the last day of camp when I had to say goodbye that he gave me proof I succeeded—

"Miss Kacie, can I give you a hug?" he asked, his big brown eyes finally showing his youthful innocence.

Tears welled up in my eyes as I knelt down and hugged him, his little arms wrapping around my neck just like in the pool, only this time he wasn't depending on me for survival. Or maybe he was. His hug was stronger than the tiny hugs you usually get from children and lasted just a second or two longer than normal.

I'd like to think that he grew up to be a nice young

man. Maybe he joined the swim team in high school; maybe he pursued a career that involved math skills. But sadly, having witnessed the challenging, unforgiving environment he was living in, I would be surprised if he was able to break out. Even I was scared of his mother.

That summer with JaShawn had a big impact on me and spring-boarded my desire to be a child psychologist. I wanted to connect with children like JaShawn—children who unfortunately were born into difficult circumstances—and have the opportunity to work with them consistently. Hopefully increase their chances of creating a different life for themselves. I wanted to make a long-term difference in their lives, not just be a fond memory from camp (which I fear is all I was for JaShawn).

College 2002-2006

After my first year in college, when it was time to declare a major, I had a conversation with my dad about majoring in Psychology. He pointed out that there isn't a lot you can do job-wise with an undergraduate psychology degree so I would likely need to immediately start grad school after I graduated. He pointed out that I might not want to go to more school right away, so I should consider picking up a second major just in case. I thought it was sound logic, so I did.

I had no idea what else I wanted to do though. I remember visiting the career center at school and it wasn't any help. Ultimately, I made the decision based on what I was good at—I knew I was a decent writer and speaker, so I chose the College of Communications. Within that major, there were four emphasis areas to choose from. One of them you had to apply to get into, and being the competitive individual that I am, I applied for that one. And I got in. So I picked up a second major—Communications with an emphasis in Public Relations.

As I got into my Communications classes, I became more intrigued with the PR world—hosting events and dealing with the media—and my plan when graduating college changed from going to more school to pursue becoming a child psychologist to working in PR for a couple of years and then later going back to school to get my PhD in Psychology. Looking back on it, I think that decision set me down this path of least resistance, instead of putting me on the more difficult path towards the dream I had of connecting with children like JaShawn. It started me down the path of going where I was wanted, not necessarily where I wanted to go.

After graduating college, I got a job with a PR firm and moved to Ft. Lauderdale. I was in my early twenties, living less than a mile from the beach, and representing clients in areas like high-end jewelry, private aviation, luxury real estate, and football stadiums. My weeks were spent planning events, pitching TV stations, and attending jewelry photo shoots in luxury hotels; and my weekend routine was bouncing around popular bars—Friday nights at Tarpon Bend and Dicey Riley's; Saturdays on the beach and then into Blondies; and Sundays recovering by watching movies and ordering delivery food. Life was good.

2008 - 2009

About two years into that first job out of college, two things happened—the economy started to tank and I got restless. We lost a couple of clients due to budget cuts and I started to feel uneasy about helping these companies that catered to the rich make even more money. I felt like I should be contributing to the greater good in some way.

But once again, I had no idea what I wanted to do. I started to look into Psychology PhD programs (as had been the plan) and I took the GRE exam. I even sent out for a couple applications and started to fill some out, but I never completed them. They would all require me to move away from my life in Ft. Lauderdale where I was comfortable with my friends and my social routine. That would have been another difficult road.

It was around this time that I looked into joining the Peace Corps. I had always wanted to go to Africa and I thought this would be the perfect way to do it. I remember bringing it up to my mother and her freaking out. "Two years is a long time." "It's dangerous." "How will that break affect your ability to get a job when you get back?" "Do you really want to be away from your family and friends for that long?" She got me with that one. I remember thinking that if it was only one year I would do it, but two years would be too long—think of everything I would miss out on in those two years.

I even tried to become a writer. Well, kind of. I had an idea that I legit pitched to several national magazines—quitting my job and moving to Europe and documenting the whole thing as a column. Think *Sex & The City* meets *Eat, Pray, Love.*

Clearly, none of the magazines I pitched went for it and obviously I didn't actually end up quitting my job and moving to Europe. Instead, I quit my job for a marketing position with a health care system. A friend of mine's sister was the VP of marketing for the system—at a family dinner, she mentioned they had a position open. My friend knew I wasn't happy in my job, so he offered my name up and got the information on how to apply. I applied, was offered the job, and I accepted. I felt better about that job because while I might not be helping people directly, at least the organization I worked for would be. But did I pursue that job because it was what I wanted? Nah. I took that job because the opportunity came along and they wanted me.

Again I went where I was wanted, not where I wanted to go. (Ugh, this pattern...)

2011 on

I was recruited by a competing health system for a physician sales job. I was later fired from that job for failing to report a conflict of interest. That conflict was getting into a relationship with one of the physicians in my territory... a married physician—my "other woman" story. I then went back to the first health care system in a sales role for a couple years before I met Shane, the boyfriend I moved back home to Jacksonville for.

In the years that followed, I stopped entertaining the big ideas I had before. My life simply continued on unquestioned... until now.

Until that damn YouTube video asked me what my purpose was and resurrected all these memories and feelings I must have buried deep down.

JOURNAL ENTRY: a walk off track, *part 2*

MARCH 2017

April listened intently as I relived all my career choices. I confessed that I was feeling angry at my parents for their reactions to my ideas, even though I ultimately knew that every decision I made was my choice... and I could have chosen differently.

But that's the thing—it's like I never really chose. I just passively went along with what other people suggested or where people wanted me to go. I feel like I never really actively pursued something.

I know I didn't apply to UNC Chapel Hill out of fear of rejection. I remember that clearly. But what about everything else? Why didn't I pursue the PhD in Psychology? Or join the Peace Corps? Was it also a fear of rejection... a fear of failure? Or was it just an overall lack of awareness of what I (emphasis on *I*) wanted?

Now I was feeling angry with myself.

April cautioned me not to be so hard on myself. "It doesn't matter that you got off track," she said as we neared the end of our walk. "It all brought you to where you are today. And where you are today is getting back on track."

JOURNAL ENTRY: driving directions

MARCH 2017

Back when I accepted my new job in HR in the construction industry, I actually had two offers and was faced with a career choice—I could either stay on my current career path in sales and take a job that would be a natural next step, or I could make a career change and do something slightly less prestigious but in my mind had the potential to open all kinds of doors for me in the future.

Amidst my interviews with the two companies, my dad reached out to me wanting to discuss the choices, so I went over to my parents' house one night to talk about them. I knew the career change option concerned him. I went over there really hoping for a two-way conversation with him equally looking at both options. I didn't want him to stay firm on what he thought was best for me; I wanted him to *hear* me, to understand my points and consider them.

I tried so hard not to get emotional in that conversation, and to logically explain to him why I thought the career change—HR in the construction industry—was a better option for me, even though (to be honest) I didn't really know why I thought it was. I just felt like it was. I even tried to play up aspects that I thought he could relate to... "It will add dimension to my resume, better positioning me for management jobs in the future." "I'll be part of the leadership team of a growing company."

But the conversation did not go how I wanted it to. The choice was clear to him. Why wouldn't I take the job that I already had the skillset for? I didn't know anything about HR or construction. (Both valid points.) But also, why wouldn't I take the job where I had the potential to make significantly more money? I didn't know what to say to that one. I couldn't look my father in the eye—the man who had given me an incredible life where I grew up in a great house, went to private school, didn't have to pay for college, and went on family vacations to the Bahamas, yet somehow managed not to come out a spoiled brat due to the values they instilled in me—and tell him that money might have been his priority in life, but it wasn't mine. There's no way to say that without it sounding insulting, and insulting my father was the last thing I wanted to do.

I left that conversation upset and flustered that it wasn't the two-way conversation I had hoped for.

It was actually the hiring manager for the sales job that gave me a great mental exercise to try to help me figure out what to do. I was very honest with him regarding my concerns about taking the job he was offering me—mainly that, as I explained it, it would be the same dog and pony show I was currently in, just with a different dog and a different pony. He understood my concerns and immediately went into mentoring mode—as opposed to sales mode to try to convince me to take it, which I would have expected him to do. He was the VP of sales after all. But instead, he told me to think of a time in my career (or life) when I felt really good; a time when everything was clicking, and I was firing on all cylinders. Then he told me to dissect that time period to decipher what my success drivers were. To do that, he said to consider three questions:

1. **WHAT EXACTLY WAS I DOING?** Not what industry or what job, per se, but was I following procedures that had already been established, or was I building something from the ground

up? Was I responsible for one main function or many? Was I accomplishing a lot of tasks or doing more analytical work?

2. **WHAT WERE THE DYNAMICS?** Was I an individual contributor or doing group work? Was I part of team or leading a team?

3. **WHAT WAS MY ENVIRONMENT LIKE?** Was I in an office all day, or for part of the day, or working from home? Did I have a lot of meetings with others or was I working by myself most of the day?

He explained that people too often choose career moves based on the role or industry they've previously been successful in, so they think they'll be successful in a similar role or industry. But what really matters are the answers to those questions—the things that drive you. I loved that exercise because it involved logic and thinking instead of the "listen to your gut" advice I so often got.

I'll admit I struggled with doing that exercise. It was hard to think of a time when I was firing on all cylinders. Maybe I never have been. I ultimately took the HR job because of something a friend said to me. When I told her the story of how the President and CFO of the company had asked me to come be their

HR manager, she pointed out an interesting way of looking at it. She said, "Here's two people who don't know you very well and know you don't have any HR experience, yet they still want you for the job. There's something they see in you. I don't know, but I think that's pretty cool." When I thought about it like that, it *was* pretty cool.

But thinking about it now, it's once again just another example of me going where I was wanted instead of figuring out where I wanted to go. (face-palm)

However, there are several things about this career move that energize me and fall in line with my answers to the questions above—as the first HR person the company has ever had, I'm building something (the HR department) from scratch. I'm part of the leadership team. I don't love being in an office all day, but at least I love everyone else in the office—they're down-to-earth and don't take everything so seriously. It's much less stuffy than the more corporate environments I've been in, where we'd have meetings to discuss meetings and Bcc was used like a nuclear bomb in email warfare.

At this point, only a couple of weeks into the new job, I think I made the right decision. But do I feel deep down in my gut that this is it for me? That this is what

I'm meant to do? Nope. But similar to me giving up men for Lent, something had to change career-wise for me. I couldn't keep going down the path laid out in front of me, so I took a big side-step. If anything, hopefully this side-step will open up some new paths.

When I first moved back to Jacksonville, I remember loving that it's small enough to really be somebody here. Back then, I had intentions of doing a lot of networking and getting involved in civic organizations to try to be well-known in the city like my mother is. But then one day a couple of months ago, an interesting thought popped into my head— *Life isn't about being somebody; it's about the number of somebodies your being matters to.*

I love that reframe but it was a totally random thought. And out of nowhere. Where did it come from? Maybe it was my subconscious trying to wake me up to the fact that I had gotten off track. That I wasn't focusing on what I really wanted to do...

I wasn't focusing on my purpose.

I want to matter to people in a real, significant way. It's not that I want to be important, per se, but I want to play an important role in people's lives... to make their lives better. While this career move probably isn't what I'm meant to do forever, hopefully it has at least set me in the right direction to get back on track.

JOURNAL ENTRY: growing pains

MARCH 2017

I've stopped putting the news on in the morning when I get ready for work and instead I put on the motivational YouTube videos. Me—who has been making fun of this stuff for as long as I can remember. I can't help but laugh at the irony. But I no longer want to start my day off with all the problems of the world. I'd rather start it with something positive. These videos make me think of the potential for my day and for my life, and that's much more enjoyable than listening to seven people analyze Trump's latest tweet.

I'm still surprised at how much I'm enjoying them. I started adding ones I really like to a playlist and I follow the channels that post good ones—Motiversity, Be Inspired, Live Today with Passion, Absolute Motivation, DELEON Motivation. I've found I'm happier throughout the day. Of course, I don't know whether to attribute the happiness to the videos or more to my overall awareness and determination to overcome this existential crisis... but either way, I'll take it.

As I write this, I wonder *what is the actual definition of existential crisis?* Well, according to the all-knowing Wikipedia, it is:

"... a moment at which an individual questions the very foundations of their life: whether this life has any meaning, purpose, or value. It is commonly tied with depression and/or a feeling of a lack of purpose in life."

Yep, that about sums it up.

I really should have seen this coming. In the beginning of this year, I told some friends and my parents that I had figured something out about myself—"I'm addicted to challenge," I told them. It explains why I wanted to run a marathon, why I got my MBA, and it certainly explains some of the men I've dated. They all agreed and I really thought it was this big revelation about myself. But I was only halfway to the real revelation.

At my previous job, our weekly department meetings always started off with one of the directors sharing some kind of motivational insight from a management book or leadership skills exercise. I hated those huddles (as they were called) because they were usually awkward and not impactful. I thought it was a stupid and pointless waste of time. So before I left that job, when my boss asked me to start off our team meeting in a similar fashion, I was determined to make it actually meaningful.

While doing some Googling to find something to talk about, I came across the following quote—"A comfort zone is a beautiful place, but nothing ever grows there." I connected with it immediately because taking on new challenges is a way to break out of your comfort zone. I decided to use the quote for the team meeting. I found a cool picture of a lizard shedding its skin to reveal a new layer of beautiful, brightly colored skin, and I talked about the importance of pushing ourselves outside of our comfort zones to learn new things, grow, etc.

Grow. That was the real revelation. It was right in front of me but at the time I didn't connect it all; I didn't see it. But I do now.

It's not so much the challenge that's important; it's the growth that results from overcoming that challenge. Each challenge I've tackled forced me out of my comfort zone for sure. But what was the growth that really resulted from it?

I wasn't the stellar student I wanted to be in my MBA program. I excelled in the social aspect of it, but I wouldn't say I came out the other side with much tangible, valuable, new business sense that would help grow my career. In fact, nothing changed career-wise for me after I graduated, and my MBA was not at all a factor in me getting my new job. I didn't really grow from tackling that challenge. Probably because that wasn't the challenge I had deep down always wanted to pursue. For so long, I wanted to be a psychologist—dealing with people and analyzing thoughts and emotions. But I headed down this career path that took me so far from that desire that I forgot about it. My career had put me in the business world, so naturally I got a Master's in Business Administration—dealing with transactions and analyzing numbers. That couldn't be further from a PhD in Psychology!

Maybe I didn't really grow from it because I was never really connected to it to begin with.

The marathon pushed me out of my comfort zone both physically and mentally. Obviously running 26.2 miles is physically uncomfortable, but more importantly it showed me that I have the mental discipline and strength to push myself further than most people ever choose to. While that's awesome, when you think about it, it really just points out that I'm capable of a lot more than what I'm currently doing. I have a level of mental discipline and strength that I don't utilize on a daily basis.

So basically, the big challenges I've tackled, as impressive as they might seem to others, didn't provide me with what's really important. I didn't really grow from them. If anything, they highlighted my unreached potential to grow. No wonder I didn't feel the satisfaction I wanted from them. I'm not addicted to the challenge itself; I crave the growth that's supposed to result from it.

It explains why I get restless with a job after I master it. It explains why I feel restless in my life overall. These videos constantly talk about going after your dreams in a very intentional way—writing down your goals and making a plan to achieve them. It seems so basic and obvious, but I haven't been doing it. I haven't had any goals written down. I haven't even had any goals formulated in my head! I'm sure there have been things I've wanted to do over the years, but I can't remember what they were.

No wonder I've been feeling so off. I didn't know why I was here and I don't have any goals. *Geez la weez.* I thought I had my shit together but really I've just been aimlessly wandering through life.

Well that clearly has to change.

So in an effort to find out where and how I can grow... no, no—where and how I *want* to grow... I've started writing down some goals. When I get ready in the morning (yes, with my trusty videos playing in the background), if I think of something I used to dream of doing and still feel like I want to do, I'll now run into my bedroom and write it down on a notepad I found in my nightstand drawer. I only have a couple of goals so far:

- Write a book
- Go to Africa
- Get (and stay) out of credit card debt
- Start a company that helps children get out of poverty

It feels good to even just think about all the possibilities; to think back to all the things I've thought about doing—even going back to when I was a child—and contemplate really going after them. It feels like I'm getting back in touch with myself.

JOURNAL ENTRY: writing my wrongs

MARCH 2017

Tonight, I crawled into bed and picked up my notebook to elaborate on my goals:

- Write a book—this is something I've always wanted to do and I don't really know why. Over the years, I've had several ideas on what my book could be about—usually something relationship-oriented and always real life, not fiction. I've even sat down to start writing a couple of the ideas, but never made it past a page or two. I guess those ideas just weren't my book, or maybe I just wasn't ready yet.

- Go to Africa—this has been a dream since childhood. Growing up, Sunday nights were spent watching the Discovery Channel together in the family room while eating our dinner from TV trays. Looking back, I realize it was kind of a funny tradition—eating dinner while watching lions rip apart zebras. But it was what we did and we loved it. And I loved the animals. Sometimes I would dream of being a large animal vet, or a wildlife photographer... but the one thing I knew I had to do was go to Africa to see in person the animals I loved so much.

- Get (and stay) out of credit card debt—Soooooo I haven't always been the best budgeter. And by that I mean historically I haven't budgeted at all. It started when I first moved to Ft. Lauderdale out of college and was pretty much being paid in jelly beans, yet I just had to live by the beach and live a social lifestyle that my jelly beans (sadly) couldn't support. When I finally dug myself out of that hole, a three-month stint of unemployment pushed me into another hole. After clawing my way out of that one, I bought a condo in Ft. Lauderdale only to decide to move back to Jacksonville less than a year later, and I couldn't quite sell that condo as quickly as my heart made me move. Paying a mortgage plus rent for six months was no fun. I only have a small balance left, but I'm tired of the ups and downs. I just want to pay it off, be better about budgeting for things I want to do, and be done with it. Recognizing budgeting isn't my strong point, I finally wised up and got a financial advisor when I moved back to Jacksonville to help keep me more accountable.

- Start a company that helps children get out of poverty—this dream, not surprisingly, started with JaShawn. That summer with him gave me a new understanding of the power of the cycle of poverty. I knew enough about the neighborhood he was growing up in to know his childhood lessons mostly consisted of negativity, fear, violence, hatred, and blame. Who was going to teach him (or even just show him) the values one needs to succeed in life? How can we expect children like him to grow up to be productive members of society without some help?

I thought about all of this for a minute, pondering if those really were my goals.

Starting a company will be very hard. Where will I find the financial resources? Should I forego that idea and instead try to be successful in an already established company that works with underprivileged children?

And there it was again. I didn't even notice it. It's so easy to choose the easier path, the "normal" next step, the go-with-the-flow path of least resistance. It's like our brains are wired to keep us in our comfort zone.

I thought about JaShawn and pictured myself starting a company that could really help children like him, and I smiled as my gut chimed in *yes, that is my goal.*

In the front of the notebook that housed my goals, there were several pieces of paper folded and stuffed in between two pages. I could tell they had been there a while. Not really having any clue what they were, I began to open them one by one.

The first was an envelope with my grandmother's handwriting on the front of it, telling my dad that there were potentially valuable stamps inside. She wrote, "Do you know anyone collecting stamps? Perhaps Kacie in the future?" And sure enough, in the envelope were two even older envelopes with stamps on them from 1948. And a sticky note that said, "Collector's item?" I thought for a minute about how many instructional notes my parents found on items in her condo after she passed away. It was so hard for them to go through all her stuff, constantly finding these messages explaining the story behind things or the significance of her belongings. I guess the desire to leave behind your stories gets even stronger towards the end.

I thought back to the enormous bag of stamps she gave me as a child that belonged to my grandfather—very few actually organized in a stamp collector's book. It was just an old shopping bag full of old envelopes and Christmas cards, most of them torn so that just the part with the stamp was left. Several years ago, when

I was unemployed for months after being fired for the married doctor situation, I went through all those stamps and categorized them while daydreaming that maybe there was a stamp in there worth millions and I would never have to work again. I even sought out an official stamp collector—a sweet old man I met at the public library so he could inspect my collection. I remember the disappointment I felt when he kindly said, "There likely isn't any value in here other than the fun your grandfather had collecting them." It was like he knew I was looking at the stamp collection through the wrong lens. A typical, ungrateful granddaughter not being appreciative of the sentimental valuables left behind for her.

I ended up taking those stamps and mod-podging them on coffee mugs for each of my family members and even extended family on my mom's side who had gotten to know my grandmother after years of Christmas Eves spent together. For each mug, I tried to pick out stamps that pertained to that family member—hobbies, where they were from, where they went to college, etc. I wonder if anyone still has those mugs. For myself, I made coasters that I still use and I put some in a framed collage that's currently hanging next to my bed. So there, sweet old stamp collector—I kept the nostalgia alive.

The next unfolded piece of paper was a Thanksgiving prayer I wrote many years ago. Every Thanksgiving, we take turns on who writes the prayer. This one focused on the importance of family. I felt a pang of guilt as I read it and wondered again why I feel so disconnected from this family that I've been so close to my entire life.

The last two papers were folded-up, kids' paper placemats from Shooters, a restaurant in Ft. Lauderdale where I was a part-time hostess on evenings after work and on the weekends. I got that job a year or so after I moved down there because my credit card balance had gotten higher and higher, proving my dad right—his reaction to me telling him about my first job offer was, "How are you going to live off that salary?" Parade rained on. But once again, Dad correct.

This hostess job was right around the time I started to feel unhappy in my PR job but didn't know what I wanted to do next. I had a lot of time to think on weeknights at that hostess stand. Sometimes I would get a thought process going that had a nice rhythm to it and I would write it down. I did this relatively frequently during those years of my life—I would write... I guess you could call them poems. It was never very intentional—I would just randomly find my mind creating them while I was running or driving, and I would hurry to write them down or type them up before I forgot the words. I don't write them anymore. The last one I wrote was about four years ago. It was about friendship and travelling the road less travelled. I printed it on nice paper and gave a copy to my three best South Florida friends at our Friendsgiving dinner.

I opened the first kids' paper placemat—there were a couple of short notes on a book I'd thought about writing about my relationship with JaShawn and that experience as a camp counselor.

Below those notes was the following:

been in PR
I want to make a difference
> *help people*
> *drive home and feel good about my day's work*
> *wake up excited to go to work*
> *have pride in what I do*
> *make career out of passion - people*

Reading that stung a little. I guess I did used to write down goals... but they somehow got lost. They were sitting stuffed inside a random notebook all this time while I was out and about sleeping with a married man and deciding what drink to order. (sigh) All

those things that were important to me but then I
didn't really pursue. I tried not to let it bother me,
focusing instead on how I was getting back on track.

And then I opened the next kids' paper placemat.
Written in my oftentimes only-legible-to-me blend
of cursive and print, with parts scratched out and
rewritten as I struggled to find the right words, was
the following:

the truth is I don't know
what I knew is gone and what I should know has changed
the truth is I'm scared
scared for where I'm going and scared for where I've been
the truth is I'm lost
lost in feelings I should be feeling and decisions I never made
the truth is I'm tired
tired of the questions and guesses and gambles
the truth is I'm angry
angry at the things I should have done and the things I
know I'll do
the truth is I'm unsatisfied
unsatisfied with a life meeting expectations set by others and
potential set by me
the truth is I'm happy
happy with the day and happy for the moment

I sat there stunned for several minutes. I even said,
"oh my gosh" out loud to myself. I couldn't believe I
had written that back then. I recalled the memory of

writing it, a memory that hadn't surfaced in years—I was standing at that hostess stand, writing those words and feelings, and not at all understanding where they were coming from, but just needing to get them out of my head and onto paper.

In what was probably slow motion due to shock, I flipped over to the other side of the placemat, where there was another one I'd written that same night.

what if no one is who they say they are and we never
meet ourselves
what if there is no winner in the games we play
no ties and no overtime, but instead a constant game that we
shouldn't be playing
what if the fears that we struggled for so long to bury deep in our
souls are destined to rise back to the surface
what if the anger never fades and the bitter tears never dry
what if we never find the answers to the questions because the
answers were always there and what we thought we knew was
actually what we should have been questioning
what if the chemistry is all chemical and no emotion
what if you can't open up to someone else until you open
up to yourself
what if the connections are broken when we move and the distance
only closes when we're gone
what if there is no perfect ending, no how it was supposed to be,
no worked out for the best
what if it just ends
all we have is this moment

a brief fleeting moment that holds timeless truth
the past may be set in stone but the lessons learned change shape
and color until the facts are blurred and the influence of our
imperfect memory erases the knowledge gained
the future is uncertain constant motion affected by our
every decision
it cannot be guessed. cannot be predicted. it can only be gambled.
but this moment is ours. this moment is now. but only for
this moment.

Holy shit. It was like my 24-year-old-self predicted the future. Like she knew the steps off track had gotten too big and weren't going to stop. She had all the questions about life back then that I have now. She literally took the feelings right out of me—like the me of today time travelled back to that night at Shooters, took her pen, and wrote those words. I read them both again out loud. I needed to hear my 32-almost-33-year-old-self verbalize the feelings of my 24-year-old-self. I couldn't tell if I never felt more connected to that version of myself than in that moment, or if she had made a fool out of me. I felt this way back then and did nothing about it other than scribble some words on a paper kids' placemat. Tears welled up as the realization that I had wasted almost ten years of my life set in.

It's so obvious to me now that things are very meaningful to me. I'm not this hardened, jaded person—I'm the person who mod-podges old stamps on coffee mugs for her family; I'm the person who writes Thanksgiving prayers about family; I'm the person who wants to write a book about a little boy who touched her heart when she was a teenager. I write goals. I write poems. It's all so deeply analytical and meaningful. And where is all that depth and meaning in my life now?? It doesn't exist.

Somewhere along the way, I lost that part of me. No wonder I feel so disconnected.

JOURNAL ENTRY: coming a little clean

MARCH 2017

My mind still blown from the writings last night, I started thinking about what was going on in my life when I worked at Shooters. Why would I feel that way at 24 years old when, by all societal standards, I was having so much fun? And I *was* having so much fun. (I think...)

I've never admitted this before but one reason I enjoyed the hostess job was that it gave me a legitimate reason not to go out. My friends couldn't give me a hard time about not going out because I had to work. It was an uncomfortable feeling of enjoyment for me, as I was still in the throes of my party days. I was a regular at the bar. I knew the bartenders by name and vice versa. I hesitate to say it was my identity... but it might have been. No one would understand why I wouldn't want to go out, or at least that's what

I assumed. Probably because I barely understood it. I remember lying to my best friends Amber and Taylor one Halloween about getting off work later than I actually did because I didn't want to meet them out at the bar. They came home that night drunk and loud. I stood in the kitchen with them laughing, but deep down feeling a little annoyed, and wondering what was the point of being in that state. Then I got upset with myself for being annoyed. I felt so conflicted.

I began doing that more often—finding legitimate reasons not to go out to the bar. Work was a popular one.

I also used to convince Amber, my roommate, that we should do a "month of cleanse." One month with no alcohol. We'd both gotten into a more regular fitness routine so it was easy to position it as a weight loss strategy. And considering we were both broke, I could easily throw in the money saving component as well and no one would ever think it was because I didn't want to go out. I remember sitting on the couch one Friday night doing laundry and watching a movie, and Amber complaining about how boring it was. I agreed, all the while actually really enjoying it.

It's not that I didn't have fun going out; I just think I was tired of *always* going out. But I never took the time to dig a little deeper and try to understand why I felt that way. What was it that I wanted to do instead of going out to the bar? What was my life missing that I wanted?

Nor did I honor my feelings by just deciding not to go out without making up an excuse. Why didn't I give those thoughts more attention? Why was I afraid to tell my friends if I didn't want to go out? Was I really that insecure that I couldn't just say how I really felt?

I guess so.

And I'd be lying if I said I'm not still that way sometimes. There are many times when I don't really want to go out... but I do... and at first, I'm bored and not really having fun. And then I drink enough that it becomes fun. And the next day I feel awful and wish I hadn't gone out. When you think about it, that's a pretty pointless routine. Recently I've chalked those feelings up to age, telling myself I'm just growing out of the bar phase. But finding those writings and remembering how I used to find excuses not to go out proves it isn't all age. Whatever it is has always been there; I just ignored it.

I definitely have fun drinking. But there's also always been a part of me that envies the people who are happy not going out to the bar at night; they don't feel like they're missing out on anything, or being lame when they go to bed early and get up the next day to work out or do some fun activity outdoors. They don't have this unsettling marriage between drinking and having fun. They are the people who sit at coffee shops reading or kayak during the day. They are probably the same people who sat on grassy hills reading in college. Meanwhile I'm usually somewhere with a drink in hand. (sigh)

JOURNAL ENTRY: write on

MARCH 2017

I've always been jealous of people who knew exactly what they wanted to be—"I'm going to be the COO of a hospital" "I'm going to be an obstetrics nurse practitioner." Or even those people who took their passion and found a career in it. Like David. Or my friend Amber who loves skin care and has been in skin care sales for years. I can't tell you how many times as an adult I've said in a joking manner (but feeling totally serious) that I'm still figuring out what I want to be when I grow up. I remember always thinking *I wish I had a passion I could make a career out of.*

After work today, I went for a walk on the beach with my friend Rachel. It was the typical girl talk— dating and job. The job part took an interesting turn though, as she's also struggled with the "what do I want to be when I grow up" question. She talked about an interest in health coaching or maybe being an aesthetician. Then she came out of the blue with wanting to be a pastry chef. She immediately dismissed the idea, saying she would have to quit her job and go to culinary school and that's not going to happen. I stopped her right there and tried to harness my inner motivational speaker. I told her that too often we focus on why we *can't* do something instead of all the reasons we *should* or *want* to. She listened and agreed, but I could tell she didn't really hear me. And I don't blame her—I was struggling to get my point across. My motivational speaker skills clearly need some work.

We reached our turn-around point and it was time to talk about me. Gulp. As we walked back up the beach, I told her what I've been going through and thinking about over the past couple weeks. I started from the beginning point of being so disturbed after listening to the "what is your purpose" video. I told her about how I've continued to listen to motivational videos and started to write down goals. I told her about the writings I found and even read one to her from my phone. She was interested but didn't really seem as mind-blown as I've been. I found my brain sneaking back into its old habits and trying to pull me back to my comfort zone... *you're being over-dramatic... this is not a big deal... nothing is really happening to you... your life is fine how it is...*

On the walk back, Rachel managed to plug in the pastry chef idea a couple more times. Always in passing. But I couldn't let it go when she mentioned it one last time as we reached her car parked outside my apartment. I told her she could start to pursue that dream without completely turning her life upside down. I mentioned a couple of local schools that have culinary programs. I tried as much as I could to encourage her to just consider it—to just take the first step. But I could tell she didn't see it as a step; all she saw were all the obstacles.

Why don't we all just go after what we really want to do? Why do we question the voice inside us that says, "I want to be _____"? It's like we're programmed to think that only children can have those dreams. And then those childhood dreams get squashed by the reality of adulthood.

And we're just supposed to accept that.

But if that's the case, what was the point of the dreams? Why did anyone even ask us what we wanted to be when we grew up? It shouldn't have been an open-ended question. It should have been a multiple-choice question with only a list of jobs society deems "possible" as answer options. But does it really have to be that way? I vote *no*. We can make our childhood dreams come true. And even if we've forgotten what our childhood dreams were, we can figure it out now and make those dreams come true. Or even find new ones. It's never too late.

And now, as I sit here in the midst of my existential crisis, I should probably turn that thought process towards me. What were my childhood dreams? What do I really want to do and why am I not pursuing it?

Considering the different writings I've found, I guess it seems clear that I knew my passion, but I lost sight of it—maybe because it wasn't as specific and concrete as other people's, or maybe because I didn't have the strength or self-awareness to pursue it.

My passion is people; connecting with people and helping to make their lives better on some level.

And my passion is writing. I've always done it—I wrote cute little poems that rhymed as a kid. When the neighbor down the street who I didn't even know died, I wrote his widow an anonymous poem and put it in her mailbox. When Princess Diana died, I wrote a poem for William and Harry and submitted it on some website that allowed you to send condolences.

I've written who knows how many letters to friends and family... and ex-boyfriends. My first paper in college was nominated for a first-year writing award. I love quotes. I get probably a little too much satisfaction when I think of a clever Facebook status update or picture caption. I send long text messages. Writing is and always has been my preferred way to express myself.

Write a book. It's right there listed as a goal but I've never thought of it in terms of being a career. It's always just been something I'm good at and enjoy doing. But hello!? Aren't those the exact two qualifications for making a career out of your passion? Holy shit. Is "author" my answer to what I want to be when I grow up?

I've always wanted to write a book but I could never find my voice and the right avenue in which to use it. I didn't know my story or what I wanted to say. Until now. I know I can't be the only one feeling this way. I'm not the only one unsatisfied in a "happy" life. I'm not the only one who inexplicably craves something different for their life... craves something more.

This is my book.

I don't know where it will lead. I don't know the end

of the story. I just know the story is my story—how I was feeling and how I'm trying to change it... and the rest is a mystery at this point.

But what is no longer a mystery is what I want to be when I grow up. I want to be an author... an author whose books connect with people and make their lives better. And just like in the movie *When Harry Met Sally*, when Harry says, "When you realize you want to spend the rest of your life with somebody, you want the rest of your life to start as soon as possible," I feel the same way about realizing what you want to do with your life... you want it to start as soon as possible. It's finally time for me to grow up.

JOURNAL ENTRY: intentional judgment

MARCH 2017

I talked to my mother while I was at work today but the conversation felt off to me. Like I was keeping something from her. I guess in a way I am. She knows about my Lenten promises but I haven't told her about the YouTube video, or the writings I found, or my new life plan. We are getting together this weekend, with my dad also, and I'm struggling with how much to tell them about what I'm currently going through and everything I've been thinking about. When I try to pinpoint why I'm hesitating to tell them, I guess the reason is that I expect them to judge me—not in the sense that what I'm feeling is wrong, but in the sense that they'll chalk it up to something else— "She's lonely." "She's sad that Kimberly is pregnant." They're going to try to make something the root of, or reason for, my feelings—when really, my current thoughts and feelings are a byproduct of me losing touch with my true self, not pursuing my own life. But they'll think I'm having some early mid-life crisis, desperate to fill the void of not having a man. I just don't see how they'll understand.

I can picture my dad's face, trying so hard to hide a smirk that would reveal the thought going through his mind—*Stop being so over-dramatic.* As smart as he is, and as similar as our brains are, I can't imagine him truly understanding this. He is so logical. And unfortunately, logic these days doesn't really lend itself to pursuing big dreams like becoming an author. Logic usually tells you to stay on the safe path... the predictable path.

And I can picture my mother too—her face overcome with emotion and confusion while her mind runs in circles trying to figure out what she did wrong... *Have I been talking about Kimberly or Courtney too much? Have I not asked her about her life enough? Have I asked her about her life too much?* She tells me time and time again that all she wants is for me to be happy and she means it to her core. But I'm not sure she understands what *my* happiness looks like. Lately I feel like she's so sad for me. She'll ask me what I did the past weekend and when I don't have any exciting news to tell her— when I tell her I stayed in or laid low—she says, "Oh, okay," in this voice that's trying so hard to sound happy and normal but the undertones of sadness and pity are unmistakable.

She thinks I need to be out at the bar to be living the normal, fun, single life. Not even just single life—she thinks that's what couples do for fun too. And to her point, it often is. And historically, I have been that single person and I have been one of those couples. And I wasn't happy. But it's not her fault I never told her. It's not her fault I only did what I secretly wanted to do when I could cower behind a "legitimate reason" not to go out.

Still I find myself feeling angry towards my parents for every look or tone or rebuttal that didn't fully support a decision I wanted to make or had already made. Their intentions were always looking out for what they thought was the best for me... and to their credit, I have made some stupid decisions that any parent would have a hard time watching without speaking up (ahem, married man, ahem). But still I just wanted them to support me; to trust me and my choices.

I can't tell them that though. It will crush them. They'll blame themselves for my current unhappiness. And when I really think about it... when I'm really being honest with myself... there is no one to blame but me. I gave those looks, tones, and rebuttals the power to impact my decisions; to overpower what I wanted deep down. *I did that.*

It's an odd feeling to be thankful for their intentions but at the same time resentful because of my own reaction to those intentions.

JOURNAL ENTRY: how many heads does it take

to find yourself? a 1...a 2... a 3!

MARCH 2017

The other day, my friend Hadley joined me to watch the sunrise. As we sat there chatting, she mentioned that her dad was coming into town to teach for a week at Jacksonville University, his alma mater, and while here he would be the featured speaker at a writing event the college was hosting.

Hadley and her dad are very close and I've met him twice before—first, about a year ago at an 80s themed party that Alex and Kimberly had at their house on a night when he happened to be in town. Hadley wanted to make an appearance at the party so her dad was forced to come along. I'd like to say I took the time to talk to him and get to know the father of the girl who was quickly becoming a great friend, but I didn't. I was too consumed with the drink in my hand and the guy I brought—Adam—who I wasn't sure if I was officially "dating" at that point. The second meeting was a brief encounter on my birthday at the TPC golf tournament (which is really just a big party), where I was once again more focused on drinking and meeting up with Adam, who I then *was* officially dating.

"Wait," I said, "I feel embarrassed that I have to ask this, but what does your dad do again? Or, why is he speaking?" I felt a pang of guilt as I asked. How self-absorbed have I been that I don't even know what her father does for a living? That's friendship parent info 101.

She explained that he'd be speaking about his screenplay writing. *Hmmmm, sounds like a familiar goal.* I then started to ask her all the questions I should have asked him at the 80s party. How many has he written? Have any been made into movies? Has he written any books? How many?

Turns out, he started his career in sales and then left Corporate America and started writing. He's written several books and now consults businesses and coaches executives all over the world. She could probably see the light bulb turn on in my head as I asked, "Does

he like talking to young people about their careers?"
I hadn't even told her yet that I wanted to write (or
was currently working on) a book.

"Yea he loves it," she said.

And that was that—I attended his speech on writing
last night and we had lunch today.

As we first sat down to lunch, I felt a little awkward
because I imagined he was wondering why on earth
I wanted to have lunch with him. So in true direct
Kacie fashion, I called out the elephant in the room
immediately.

"I'm sure you're wondering why I wanted to get
together with you..."

He gave me the same intense yet blank look that
Hadley gives me when she's processing what
she's thinking.

I nervously explained that when Hadley told me about
his career and specifically his decision to leave sales
to pursue writing, it really clicked with me. Feeling
somewhat vulnerable discussing this with a borderline
stranger, I forced myself to confess that I was on some
kind of self-awareness journey. I told him I felt like
life has started to present me with opportunities to

continue down this path, and I thought talking with him was one of those opportunities. I used his own words from his event speech, saying that "my head has not been aligned with my heart" and that I'm really working on that—trying to find my purpose and my passion and working towards very specific goals, one of which is to write a book. His ears immediately perked up.

Just as direct as me (which I expected), he quickly asked, "Why do you want to write a book?"

It wasn't in a curious way; it was more like a test question. I felt like I fumbled the answer, but I was honest. I inarticulately explained that it's something I've always wanted to do, but that I couldn't ever find my story. I told him about how I'd been feeling bleh and everything I gave up for Lent. I told him how I started journaling and about the old writings I found, and that it just feels like this is my book. I started to try to elaborate on everything I've been going through, but he didn't need much explanation. He nodded his head in complete understanding and told me he went through the same process when he left the corporate sales world. I felt another sigh of relief in my heart. *He understands. I'm not crazy.*

From that moment on, we were completely in sync.

He shared his insights on how we grow and change throughout our lives, and everything he said made perfect sense to me. I'll share my favorite part—

He explained how we all have three heads that we are constantly juggling throughout life. The first head is focused on the image we project out into the world— how other people see us. The second head is focused on the feedback we get back from the world—how other people react to us. The third head is who we truly are. And throughout life, we dole out different weights of importance to the different heads. In high school, we primarily care about the first and second heads. Are we cool? Are we accepted? What do people think of us? It isn't until after college that we really even know the third head exists. And at some point, some of us—not all of us—take the journey I'm on to really get to know the third head and focus less on the first and second heads. Pretty much letting the second head go altogether. I love this. It helps explain so much:

- Hiding behind work or boyfriends as excuses to not go out = my second head worried that my friends won't think I'm fun.

- My desire to post a picture when I'm doing something fun = my first head wanting to maintain my image as a party girl.

- Constantly checking a social media post to see how many likes and comments it gets = my second head wanting to be cool.

- Feeling embarrassed to tell people I left a sales job in a big company for an HR job in a construction company = my second head worried that the job snobs will look down on me.

- Feeling scared to tell my parents about all my recent realizations = my second head worried my new life will mean more distance from them.

My second head is clearly to blame for all my steps "off track." *Why has it been so dominant?* I've always been a confident person. Well, maybe more so on the outside. My first head has done an excellent job of portraying myself as more confident than my third head would say I actually am, but as I get to know my third head more, that portrayed confidence is becoming a reality.

I've decided I'm going to tell my parents a little about what's going on with me tomorrow. My second head will just have to sit this one out.

And no more excuses about why I don't want to go out. Case in point—Kimberly just texted me asking what I'm doing. It's 9:30 p.m. on a Friday night and I'm literally in pajamas in bed writing this. I responded back to her that I'm home reading. I didn't say writing because I don't want to tell a lot of people I'm writing a book yet. Maybe that's okay because it's personal or maybe that's a side effect of a fear I haven't realized yet. Oh wait, yes I have—it's a fear that I won't actually do it and people will know. My second head strikes again!

And on the second head subject, here's a big confession about social media—

I don't miss it at all. The pressure to take the perfect picture, find the perfect filter, and write the perfect caption weighed on me more than I like to admit. I used to catch myself thinking in status updates. Literally. I would be driving along and think of some witty saying and think *I need to post that.* Or on my way out to meet up with friends, I would think of the perfect photo caption to go along with the evening. I then *had* to take the perfect picture so as to not waste the perfect caption. I had different strategies I would use:

1.   "We need to remember to take a photo tonight." Planting the seed early on if I wanted someone *else* to post a picture. Used in instances where I

wasn't doing something unique enough for *me* to post it, but I still wanted people to know I was out. Or because I thought I looked particularly cute that night.

2.   "Let's take a picture." Asking a stranger to take a group photo. The problem with this strategy is that if I didn't look good in the picture the stranger had taken, I lost my shot. Maybe I could find another moment where it could pass off as normal to take another picture, but that's not guaranteed. I've never been much of a "let's take a selfie" person because I've never wanted anyone to know I just wanted to post something. I would find myself almost jealous of the girls who shamelessly took selfie after selfie until they got a good one; or the people who had no problem saying, "I don't look good in that photo, let's ask someone else to take another one." My first head would never let me say those things, even though it really wanted a good picture to post.

As I take the time to articulate all that and admit it in writing, I'm embarrassed at how pathetic it is. But I'm banking on you knowing exactly what I'm talking about. Maybe even doing it too. It's crazy how social media has influenced us. Maybe it has contributed to the dominance of the first and second heads. I'm not blaming it completely, because ultimately the onus of staying true to ourselves is always on us. But if you think about it, it is designed more for the first and second heads—status updates are a voice for your first head then people like or comment back to your second head. It's meant to connect us... but really it's just further disconnecting us from our true selves because we're so focused on what we're portraying to the outside world and how it's reacting.

Okay, that's enough—I don't want to get into a diatribe about social media. That could be an entire book in itself.

As I move more into my third head, I'm perfectly content being home in bed on a Friday night. And I don't feel the need to post anything about it. I'm working towards a bigger goal than wasting my time and money on a night out that I won't fully remember and a tomorrow that will be painful. I'm going to wake up tomorrow, go to the gym, and then go into work for a bit. I don't feel the need to prove to the digital world that I'm out somewhere doing something fun, and I don't feel the need to actually be out somewhere having "fun." *Been there, done that.* Now, it's time for more.

Hadley's dad gave me another great nugget—he said, "Don't beat yourself up, seek to understand." Seek to understand... yes. He told me for every negative, to find a positive.

So I may have let my first and second heads be my social media managers for ten years (negative)... but hey, at least I have some great pictures (positive).

JOURNAL ENTRY: cutting to the chase, *part 1*

MARCH 2017

Today was a big step for me. I talked to my parents. *Really* talked to them.

They came to see my new office and company building. I'm sure they're still struggling to understand why I left a well-known, very respected healthcare system to work for a little-known but up-and-coming commercial plumbing and mechanical contracting company.

It's Saturday so the office was empty except for me, the president of the company, and a couple of workaholic employees. I introduced them to the president and he offered to give them a tour. As they toured the impressive 120,000 sq. ft. building—with the president of the company in jeans and work boots nonchalantly explaining future growth strategies—I could feel the validation.

As we left, my dad looked at me and admitted, "It's a really big job." To which I got to say what I had wanted to since our conversation about my two job opportunities.

"You think I would have taken a not big job?" With a look that said, "You should trust me by now."

After their visit, I went over to their house for dinner and to watch the FSU basketball game. They casually asked how things are going with me and I took the opportunity to jump right into the thick of it, scared I would lose my nerve if I didn't.

I started off high-level. I explained that I've been in a very introspective place and have done a lot of thinking to define my purpose in life. I told them how I'm no longer happy with the life I've been living and that I'm going to start living the life I feel I'm supposed to.

My mother's immediate reaction was to posture up, look at me intently and say, "And what life have you been living that you *weren't* supposed to?"

It was like she was gearing up to defend me against myself. I knew I had to choose every word very carefully. One of the greatest traits about my mother is her passion. But one wrong word or statement worded incorrectly can send her down a tirade of thoughts; and you have no hope of retracting or revising what you said. You just have to ride it out and desperately try to get back on course, knowing she won't fully be listening while her rant continues in her head for a while after it's audibly over.

I was quick to explain that it's more that the decisions I've been making and the life I've been living are no longer right for me. I explained that I want to spend my time in ways that align with my purpose and I gave some examples, like drinking less and not focusing on finding a boyfriend. I told them about some of my goals, like writing a book and starting a company one day.

My dad teared up and immediately said he was proud of me and thinks it's great, with a look of pure pride on his face. That caught me off guard.

My mother needed a little bit more for her to just accept everything I was saying. "Where is your personal life in all of this?" she asked, looking a little flustered.

Hmmm... I wasn't quite sure what she meant by that,

but I assumed this goes back to her concern over me not having any fun.

I pressed back, "Define personal life."

"Oh, ya know, your friends and family," she managed to get out sounding only 75% judge-y.

"Well," I said, purposefully looking a little confused, "I'm here now with my family. I do sunrise Sundays with my friends, among other times we hang out. I'm going to see Courtney next weekend...."

"Well, I know, but..."

Now she was really flustered and I knew I made my point so I gave her what she wanted. "Of course I'm going to continue to make time for my family and friends. I just don't want to go out drinking all night... or all day. Or spend an entire day binge watching Netflix because I'm bored or hungover. Instead I'm going to spend my time doing the things that I've realized make me feel good. Like writing. Or like today, I woke up and watched the sunrise. Then I went to the gym. Then I went into work. That's very different than my Saturdays in the past, but I've really enjoyed it. And I might do it again tomorrow."

"Okay," she said with a look of pain in her eyes. She

can't argue with my happiness. "I just don't want you to shut us out."

There it was. That's her real fear. That me living a different life cuts her out in some way. I don't blame her for having that fear. I've cut her out before...

LOOKING BACK: cutting ties

2 0 0 9 — 2 0 1 1

AGE: 25 - 27

I left the PR firm for a job in marketing at a hospital. That's where I met Arlo. He worked as a technician in the lab. I remember the first time I saw him. My boss was giving me a tour of the hospital and introducing me to everyone—we popped our heads into the lab and there he was, sitting at the computer. My first thought was *WHOA*. He had dark hair, intense brown eyes, and a body you could tell was incredible even in scrubs.

Over the next couple weeks, we had a lot of sneak peeks at each other when we passed in the hallways and eye contact that lasted a little too long when we saw each other in the cafeteria. I started to find excuses to go down to the lab and eventually we started actually conversing—well, by *conversing* I mean having short, flirty conversations in the hallway.

My roommate Amber and I would laugh and strategize on how to take the conversation to the next level. There may or may not have been a strategy involving borrowing his CDs for a road trip and then making him a mixed CD as a thank-you. Yes, go ahead and laugh—I made him a mixed tape. Then one day the fruits of my labor paid off and he called my office phone. I was totally caught off guard. It was our first real conversation... and also the first time I missed a BIG red flag.

He mentioned he had an 18-month-old little girl. "Oh, that's awesome," I said. And I meant it. I've always liked kids. That wasn't the red flag.

When I asked where her mother was, he casually responded, "She's around." Weird answer, right? But did I ask more into it at the time? Nope. Because I was 25 and naïve and consumed with the fact that this was the most excited I had been about a guy since first love Lloyd.

The first time we went out to dinner, I asked a little more about his situation with his baby mama and he told me that they still lived in the same house, but that they weren't together anymore. It was temporary... until they could sell the house. I remember feeling uneasy with that information but again I didn't ask the right questions. I know I asked, "Does she know where you are right now?" and his answer was, "She knows I'm out." *Me Now* would have stood up right then and got a taxi home (yes, taxi—there was no Uber), explaining that I had no interest in getting into the middle of a situation like that. But... *Me Then* did nothing. *Me Then* was lonely. *Me Then* was desperate to get over Lloyd.

Me Then was an idiot.

A couple days later, we went out again and as we said goodbye afterwards, I told him I was uneasy about the situation. He looked me right in the eyes, put his arms around me, and told me not to worry about her—that they weren't together, it was just a temporary living situation until they could sell the house... that he hadn't felt a connection like this to someone in a long time... yada, yada, yada. And I ate it up—hook, line, and sinker.

From then on, we started communicating nonstop. He would call me from the lab several times a day because his cell phone didn't get service there so we couldn't text all the time like we did in the evenings. This was my first relationship where it seemed like we had to be in constant communication. In the beginning, I thought all the texting was exciting and fun... proof we couldn't get enough of each other. Later in the relationship, it turned into feeling like an obligation. And now, I think it's a big red flag... proof of underlying control or jealousy issues. (You live and learn.)

A couple weeks into the relationship, I started getting missed calls from unknown numbers every so often. I didn't think anything of it until one day I returned to my desk and had about three missed calls from an unknown number. *That's strange*, I thought. And then the phone started ringing again—unknown number.

I picked it up. "Hello?"

A female voice on the other end answered, "Yes, hi, um, do you know Arlo?"

I immediately started to panic. There was only one person it could be. And in my panicked state, the response I came up with was, "Arlo who?" (Smooth, I know.)

She said his last name and then explained she was reviewing the cell phone bill and saw a lot of texts going back and forth between us—she wanted to know how we knew each other.

I just hung up.

I didn't know what else to do.

I was shaking. And not just on the outside; it felt like my insides were shaking too. And my internal temperature dropped like 20 degrees. I was freezing inside. It was the first time I ever experienced that feeling and to this day I don't understand it.

That afternoon after work, Arlo came over to discuss the phone call I'd gotten. He apologized for the fact that it happened and again reiterated why I didn't need to worry about it. At that point, I should have asked a million more questions. I should have gotten clarification. I should have told him to leave. I should have ended things.

Instead I slept with him.

And it gets much worse…

A few weeks after that, I texted him one night and she responded from his phone. I couldn't forget this text if I tried—"I don't know who you are but leave Arlo alone. He has a kid and another on the way."

My stomach dropped.

I burst into tears and immediately called Amber, asking her when she would be home because I needed her. I can still picture myself—sitting on the couch, phone in hand, just shocked. I felt pain. I felt guilt. I felt sadness. I felt like a foolish little girl. (I *was* a foolish little girl.)

I'm trying to remember how I confronted him about it. I think that when he texted me the next morning I just responded, "She's pregnant???"

He had an explanation, of course. And it was weak, of course. But I naively believed it... of course.

Her name is Samantha and their relationship is sadly a common story—they started out happy but then started to fight... a lot. He said they should have broken up, but they didn't. Then for some brilliant reason, they decided to have a baby. Ya know, because that always fixes bad relationships. Their logic was that they were both getting older and both wanted kids, so time was ticking. Yes, "older." He was 38. I was 25 at the time.

Things just got worse after their daughter was born, but they tried to make it work for her sake. I guess they had one good date night and ended up sleeping together (which had supposedly stopped happening). So then of course they got pregnant again. And shockingly, things between them didn't get better. He swore they weren't still together at this point; that they had separate bedrooms in the house and lived separate lives. It was all temporary until the house sold. Oh, and just to make it that much better—she worked as a nurse in the ICU at the same hospital as us.

I don't know if I was just super naïve or if he was just very skilled at manipulating me into feeling bad for him and seeing him as the victim. I'm sure it was a combination of both. But somehow, he convinced me to stay with him... and from then on, I was in a secret relationship with a man who was still living with a woman he had one child with and another on the way.

Now up until that point, I was being pretty honest with my family about Arlo. They knew when I had a crush on him and I told them when we went out for the first time. They even knew he was older and that he had a daughter.

I even explained he still lived with the mother but in different bedrooms, and that it was really just a logistical thing of trying to sell the house. For the most part, they were understanding of all that.

Hey, it could happen.

But then I had to tell them he had another child on the way. There would be no hiding that. I explained it just as he had explained it to me—because in my mind, it made sense. It was a crappy situation, but it was understandable and wasn't his fault. (Ugh, I cringed as I wrote that.)

My parents, of course, didn't see it that way. My dad even flew down to Ft. Lauderdale in the middle of the week to take me to dinner. I thought he was coming into town for business, but I later found out his sole reason for making the trip was to try to convince me to get out of the relationship ASAP. I brushed his concern off like it wasn't a big deal and defended Arlo and his situation. But when my parents' concern started to creep into every conversation I had with them, I stopped talking to them about him. And when I found out my dad had someone at his law firm run a background check on him, I was done. In my mind, my parents were being irrational, judgmental, untrusting of me, unsupportive of me, and disrespectful of me and my right to make my own decisions.

Looking back on it, I know they were just looking out for me. And they were right. But I think we all have to live our own mistakes and learn our own lessons. And as much as they wanted to stop me from living this one, I was determined to keep going.

The whole situation with Arlo and his baby mama Samantha turned into a Lifetime Movie...

Samantha and I became weirdly obsessed with each other. She started blowing up my phone with text messages, vowing to find out who I was. They would swing from pure hatred to trying to get me to empathize with her, warning me that he wouldn't give me the emotional support I needed. At first, I would ignore her, but then I started to argue back, trying for some reason to convince her that I wasn't a bad person.

Through some Facebook stalking, I found out what she looked like so I would know if I saw her at the hospital. The first time I did was across the salad bar in the cafeteria. She was completely unaware of me as I watched her make her salad, my eyes zoned in on her pregnant belly... and then her left hand holding the cafeteria tray. On that left hand was a big, bright, beautiful diamond ring. She walked away toward the cashier and I stayed there, frozen, unable to move my feet or close my mouth... fighting back tears.

When I finally snapped out of it and looked up, there was Arlo. I gave him a death stare I didn't know I was capable of and turned and walked away. When I talked to him later, there was of course a bullshit explanation that the ring wasn't actually an engagement ring, but instead a promise ring (pause, so you can laugh at that). And to make it worse, I bought that explanation. At that point, I was so deep into a bad situation that nothing could shake me hard enough for me to see the truth.

Not long after that, Samantha found out who I was. She came to my office and yelled at me for basically being a whore. In front of my boss. I started getting nasty looks from all the ICU nurses when I passed them in the halls. It was bad.

And it got worse.

Arlo started bringing his daughter around me but she wasn't allowed to know my name so she wouldn't talk about hanging out with me to her mother. She was too young to realize it was weird that she didn't know my name and just called me "Lady." When their son was born, Arlo came over to my apartment later that night. I remember Amber telling me she felt uncomfortable about that, like it was wrong of him. But to foolish me, I didn't think anything of it.

I thought it was a way for him to show me he cared about me. In reality, it was a way for him to distract me from realizing how F-ed up the situation was.

Samantha of course found out I spent time with her children. I mean, come on—who else could the mysterious "Lady" be? She would hate-text me frequently and I would turn it around to applauding her on what incredible children she was raising. It became a very weird relationship. Even years after Arlo and I broke up, I texted her one night apologizing for everything. She responded, recognizing that I was very young at that time and that she was happy it sounded like I had grown up a lot.

Baby mama drama aside, my relationship with Arlo wasn't a healthy one. I was always in trouble. He would get upset with me over what seemed like everything—if I was too friendly to a male coworker, if I didn't respond to his text messages, if I had to change our plans, etc., etc. I even got in trouble for things that happened and guys I dated before I even knew him! I was constantly apologizing. The only apology I should have ever given was "Sorry I was alive before we got together" as I walked out the door. Oh, and open the door back up to add—"and that I wasn't a nun." *Boy bye.*

But no, I stayed in that land of apologies. The wear and tear that took on my emotions had turned me into a shell of myself—distanced from those who loved me, distanced from the things I enjoyed doing, just distanced from everything, including myself.

Not to mention that two years had passed and... guess what? That "temporary" living situation hadn't changed.

Throughout my relationship with Arlo, I got in countless arguments with my mother. Mostly about how I wasn't talking to her about it. She just wanted to know what was going on but I had cut her out. I knew any conversation with her about it would end up being her telling me what to do, and I just didn't want to hear it.

I remember one conversation clear as day. I was in the grocery store and I was on the phone with her. We were arguing about Arlo, of course, and she said something to me that hit me like a bullet.

"I'm just not sure you have the strength to leave him."

I argued back, of course, that I didn't want to leave him but that if that day ever came then I would have the strength. But deep down, I didn't know if I believed myself. Deep down, I knew my mother was right. That comment haunted me.

After Arlo and I finally broke up, my mother and I had a couple good conversations about the situation and how at the time I just wanted her to let me live my life; how I understood why she was concerned, but I needed her to let me make my own mistakes and figure everything out for myself. I confessed that on some level, I wanted to make the Arlo relationship work just to prove everyone wrong... so that everyone would leave me alone and stop having so many strong opinions about how I lived my life. We promised each other that moving forward, she would be more understanding and less forceful with her opinions, and I would be more open and honest—I wouldn't cut her out.

But looking back on it now, I never gave my mother the validation she deserved. I always assumed she was mad I wasn't talking to her about my relationship because it meant she couldn't tell me what to do. But maybe what really hurt her was that I wasn't listening to her. Maybe it wasn't about her wanting to tell me what to do; maybe it was about her knowing I at least *heard* her. But what she didn't realize—and I didn't tell her—was that I *was* listening... I was always listening. I just never gave her the satisfaction of knowing that. I never told her how that comment about me not having the strength to leave Arlo was ultimately what triggered me to find the strength. The promise I should have made to her was that I would always hear her; and the promise I should have asked for in return was that she continue to call me out when needed.

Sadly, neither of us ended up keeping those promises to each other. I pretty much hopped out of my unhealthy relationship with Arlo right into an even worse situation...

LOOKING BACK: life in a lockbox

2011-2013

AGE: 27-29

Charlie was married. There were no ifs, ands, or buts about it, and I knew it from the very beginning. I met him when I got recruited away from my job at the hospital where Arlo worked for a physician sales job at a different hospital. Physician sales essentially means working with private practice physicians to try to get them to bring their patients to your hospital when those patients need elective procedures/surgeries. Arlo and I were still together when I started the new job. I met Charlie a couple months into it. He was a relatively new physician to a busy practice so a hot prospect for the hospital.

As I've mentioned before, I'm a quick-witted, sarcastic

person. So was he. And we clicked immediately. It was innocent at first... at least, from my perspective it was. We had really fun, witty banter but I wasn't attracted to him by any means. Plus, he was married.

Our banter, though, highlighted the fact that fun, witty banter was missing from my relationship with Arlo. It threw it in my face actually. And realizing that was the final push to get me to finally end that relationship which was way past its should-have-ended date.

There was an exact day that I knew Charlie was interested in me. I was still with Arlo, but I couldn't deny how much I was enjoying the banter with Charlie. You know that feeling of excitement when your phone dings for a text message and you hope it's from a certain person? I had that. Big time. We were texting about something work related, and then it turned into funny banter, and then it started to hint towards inappropriate banter. Now at this point, texting had started to become a normal means of communication in the workplace so it wasn't inappropriate that we were texting in general. But he said something that was borderline sexual.

A dirty mind can always recognize another dirty mind, and I've always had a dirty mind.

I put up a better fight in this situation than I had with Arlo—I refused to meet up with him outside of work several times, but a couple of conversations about his unhappy marriage, and how they'd split up before but tried to work it out for the kids, and how he never felt connected like this to anyone else, and blah, blah, blah... and I fell for it. Again.

I never cheated on Arlo. I broke up with him before anything happened with Charlie. Charlie, however, did not do anything about his own relationship status before we got together.

So once again, a Lifetime movie ensued.

His wife got suspicious after reviewing credit card bills and coming across a parking meter charge in Delray Beach (where I lived at the time) from a day when he was supposed to be doing rounds at the hospital. She confronted him and he lied. She didn't buy it.

She hired a private investigator. She got pictures of us. She got my number out of his phone and called me.

My panic response was to once again hang up.

She confronted him again... and then she kicked him out.

Over the course of about two years, he moved out, moved back in again, moved back out, and moved back in again. We rarely went places together for fear that we would be seen and spent most of our time together in his small apartment, which we jokingly called The Lockbox. She eventually found out who I was and told his boss, who then called the head of the healthcare system where I worked. I got fired for "failure to report a conflict of interest."

They started the divorce process. It got ugly. It stalled. And all the while, I stayed with him, thinking that love would conquer all and we would prove everyone wrong and end up together.

I was wrong, yet again.

It finally ended on a New Year's Eve day with me frantically running around my apartment crying, throwing everything he'd given me in a trash bag as he stood there with a look of despair on his face, having just told me he couldn't leave his children and was going back to them. And to his wife.

That New Year's Eve was a big vodka night.

I would like to say that was the end of the story, but sadly it wasn't. There was one more "reunion" and some continued communication until I finally accepted that it was over and blocked his number.

Throughout that relationship, I was quicker with the lies to my family. Obviously, I didn't want to tell them I was knowingly having an affair with a married man. Instead, I told them he was in the process of going through a divorce. In the beginning, that was completely accepted. But as time went on and his divorce wasn't finalized, they once again got more forceful with their opinions and advice. Conversations turned into arguments. One weekend at my sister's house, we got into a huge argument about it. To the point where I almost took a cab to the airport in the middle of the night to get out of there and away from everyone questioning me. When my dad looked up Charlie's divorce status on the circuit court website and confronted me about it, I flipped out and once again, I cut them out of my love life.

When that relationship ended, my mother and I again reconnected and talked about it. It was a similar conversation to the Arlo debriefing—I just wanted to live my own life, make my own mistakes, blah, blah, blah. I probably made her feel guilty for again having strong opinions on my life, when instead I should have admitted that I was wrong and had just been too weak to do anything about it.

I can't imagine what it must have been like for my parents—it was 4+ years of me in relationships that go against every moral and value they instilled in me... plus me not being honest with them. Hell, me not being honest with myself. Those years completely changed our relationship. It's like it created this gap between us. And for years, I filled that gap with a wall of dishonesty. A wall of things they dared not ask me about because they knew I either wouldn't answer or would get upset.

Maybe that's why I feel disconnected from my family lately. Maybe I haven't really closed the gap.

JOURNAL ENTRY: cutting to the chase, *part 2*

MARCH 2017

When I got home tonight, I got a text from my mother:

I love you so much and I'm so proud of you! I am very happy you are in a good place and moving forward in a good way with your life! You are the one who determines what makes you happy... not others. I just want to be there for you at every step of the way! I hope you'll let me be an intricate part of your journey of purpose.

I expected this text. Whenever my mother and I have a deep conversation, I always hear from her later... I assume it's after she's carefully dissected the conversation and questioned all of her reactions, wondering if she was supportive enough.

I responded:

Mom, you are an integral part of every part of my life. That's why it's sometimes hard to tell you things, because I care so much what you think, and it brings down all my walls and I'm rushed with emotions. A lot of those emotions I'm trying to sort through slowly, so the rush overwhelms me. I love you beyond words.

I read through what I just sent, hoping it would help explain on some level why I seem distant at times. Tears formed in my eyes as I read it. I added:

Even just texting that, I teared up and that only happens when I talk to you. It's not a bad thing. It's just because of how much I love you.

She responded:

Ok so now I'm tearing up and just so you know I'm saving this text forever! You are my heart... always have been. Sometimes I think I'm too involved with you and overstep my boundaries. I can't help it! When you hurt, I hurt; when you're happy, I'm happy. It's pretty simple. So all I want is your happiness and wherever that leads you I will be there for you.

How do you ever fully explain to a parent that the things in your life—especially the difficult or upsetting things—are not their fault? How do you explain that they can't change your feelings, and they can't protect you from the hurt anymore? It has to be impossible. I think our parents will always in some way see us as children who they must protect from any and all pain. But I think the pain is a necessary part of life.

My mom always jokes that you can't put an old head on a young body. That's so true and I think it has to be that way. Through all those years with Arlo and Charlie, my parents just wanted me to listen to them and get out. But had I done that—had I ended those relationships before they had run their course—what would have been the result? I might be sitting here still holding on to "what if" or worse, still be in some form of communication with them. Instead, I stayed in those relationships longer than anyone wanted me to, but for as long as I had to... which ultimately caused me more pain in the short-term, but hopefully offered a deeper lesson in the long run. And now I sit here knowing 100% that those men weren't for me—and not because someone else said so, but because I figured it out in my own time.

JOURNAL ENTRY: minding my failures

MARCH 2017

This morning I was thinking about failure. I can admit that—probably like many people—I've had a fear of failure for as long as I can remember. I've come a long way though, as I no longer avoid going for the things I fear I'll fail at. Well, at least not all the time. But when I was younger, I definitely avoided situations where I could fail.

When I was around 10 years old, I played on a basketball team for the YMCA. I guess I was a little tall for my age at that time (I'm by no means tall now), so my position was Center. To this day, I remember purposely staying behind my defender, pretending to be frustrated with the "great defense" just so I wouldn't be passed the ball and be expected to shoot... because I might miss. I knew I wasn't a very accurate shooter. Rather than work on it and be determined to get better, I just stayed behind that defender giving what were I'm sure were Grammy Award winning performances of frustration.

As I've grown older, I've gotten much better about avoiding failure. When I first got into running, I was hesitant to run my first half marathon, but I did it. I was nervous about applying to my MBA program, but I did it. I was scared to attempt running a full marathon, but I did it. I'm terrified about actually trying to get this book published... but I'm going to do it. I've found that the trick for me is to not let myself think about it too much. Just sign up. Just take the first step.

I still joke that I don't like doing things I'm not good at and generally avoid most of those things. But for the most part, I try not to let my fear of failure stop me from doing something outside of my comfort zone, like accept a job I have no experience actually doing.

When I think about the real failures in my life at this point, they are all character failures. I stayed with Arlo after I found out he was still living with the mother of his child. I should have asked a lot more questions and pushed further for actual answers. I stayed with him still when I found out she was pregnant with their second child. I should have ended it right then and there. But no. I stayed with him when I saw that she had a diamond on her finger. And I then accepted the explanation that, "Yes, she has a ring. It's a promise ring." What??? I should have RUN. That poor woman. I don't care what their relationship was like; she didn't deserve little 25-year-old me getting in the middle of it.

So many motivational speeches talk about how when you fail, it's how you react that matters—what you learn from it and how you keep going. Did I learn anything from my Arlo experience and "pick myself back up"? *Um no.* I turned around and fell right into the arms of a man I knew from day one was married.

I remember the exact moment when I failed myself—I literally thought *him deciding to be unfaithful to his marriage is not my problem.* I wanted to be a woman who didn't care.

I went into that situation with nothing but sex in mind. Seriously. I even told my friend Taylor that I was going to take it as an opportunity to be as uninhibited as I wanted because it was just going to be about sex. *(1) Bye-bye morals. (2) Yea right, Kacie!* I've never been the type of person who can separate sex from feelings… or who really wants to for that matter. I don't know who I was trying to be, but it wasn't me. And it clearly didn't work—it didn't take long for my "just sex" mentality to morph into love.

I carried a lot of guilt with me regarding those two relationships for a long time. What's funny is, over the years, I've never really thought about, or cared very much, what happened to either Charlie or Arlo—if they are okay or happy in their lives. And that doesn't come from a negative place. I just never really think about them. I've thought a lot about... and even dreamt about... their women and children though. What I put those women through was so wrong. And yea, yea, yea, "it takes two to tango" and the men were the ones being unfaithful... blah, blah, blah. Bullshit. I could have stopped that tango. I could have denied them the chance to be unfaithful *with me.* Maybe it still would have happened with someone else, but it happening with me was 100% in my control. I failed those women. I failed myself.

Thinking back on it, I can't believe it even happened. It feels so removed from my life now—who I am and have been for several years. But I bet it doesn't feel so removed from their lives. I bet they live with it every day. So it's only fair that I do on some level too.

I don't think that "guilt" is the right word to describe how those experiences are a part of me at this point.

It's more a sadness for what those women had to deal with as a result of me crossing paths with their husbands (or fiancés or baby daddies or whatever—the label doesn't matter). If I let go of that sadness, it's like it lessens or removes the impact on their lives from my life. That can't happen. That impact *did* happen. It was real. They can't remove it; I shouldn't either. It's like a song lyric I fell in love with a long time ago—"Our scars have the power to remind us the past was real." I have emotional scars from those relationships and I think it's only right that they remain.

The shame doesn't weigh as heavily on me now as it used to though. I used to not even be able to talk about it. I started to tell new friends as a way to force myself to deal with it. Each time someone I told didn't immediately scold me or judge me, I forgave myself a little bit. I allowed it to define me as a bad person a little bit less. But the scars are still there.

I don't think we can ever really figure out why we've done the things we've done or, for that matter, why we are the way we are. How the brain works is science—you can study it and understand how synapses work and how certain hormones are released or blocked and what emotions come from that process, etc. But how a specific *mind* works is not a science. Your mind is yours and yours alone. There is no way to study it, no way to dissect it. How you think and why you think in a particular way can never really be explained. All we can do is *try* to understand how significant events in our life might have changed us from that point on. And I think just going through that process is wherein lies the value, the therapy, the peace. Because while you will never arrive at a factual answer, along the path searching for it, you'll get to know yourself a lot better. Or at least I have.

Spoiler Alert—you may not like yourself at every turn. Consider yourself warned.

JOURNAL ENTRY: a valuable path

MARCH 2017

Well I've graduated from the compilation of motivational YouTube videos to psychology/personal growth podcasts. Same basic concept. More actual theories and science.

I say I've graduated, but really the YouTube app wasn't working on my phone for some reason so I went into my podcasts. A year or so ago, while I was laying out in the sun at my apartment complex pool, attempting to read a book I never ended up finishing, I overheard two women several chairs down talking about podcasts. I like podcasts and had started listening to some in the evenings instead of putting on the TV, so I started to eavesdrop on their conversation.

One woman was telling her friend about these

psychology podcasts she had begun listening to and was really enjoying. I eavesdropped until I got the name of the podcast and then immediately looked it up and subscribed.

But I never actually listened to one until this morning when I couldn't get YouTube to work.

The first one I listed to was titled "Level Up" and the description made it seem like it was going to be about going after your goals—leveling up your life. It was really just a sales pitch for one of their conferences. Coming from sales, I know when someone is trying to sell to me and it's a total turn-off. I wonder if people used to feel that way when I was selling to them? Probably. Anyhow, I suffered through it, hoping to at least get a nugget or two of a good idea or thought process to explore. I didn't. But I gave the podcast another chance and started listening to one on personal integrity. This one was much less sales-y. The speakers are clearly all told to weave in the in-person seminars every so often, but this speaker was much more subtle about it and she gave me a great nugget...

She was talking about values—passion, honesty, kindness, responsibility—and the importance of living your values. I started to think about my own values—growth, purpose, connection—and once again felt disappointed in myself that I spent so many years not living by them. And then she said something so relieving. And she said it so matter-of-factly. She said, "And your values change in different stages of your life." Yes! There it was—the explanation I so wanted for the life I had been living.

It's not that I wasted almost ten years of my life. I just had different values then—fun, friendships, acceptance. Just because I have different values now doesn't mean my values then were wrong. Quite the opposite—they were right and they were necessary. It was all part of my path of growth. It's not that I was always meant to be this person from day one; it's that I was always meant to grow into this person. My path... as winding and rough as it has been at times... still led me here. My values when I was out at the bar each weekend still led me to develop the values I now feel so strongly about. The process of growth is just that—a process.

And with that validation, I no longer regret my cherry bomb filled nights posted up at the bar at Tarpon Bend. After all, you can't find yourself if you never lose yourself.

JOURNAL ENTRY: talking heads

MARCH 2017

Today my sister-in-law Kimberly got great news—her hormone levels are rising as they should, and everything looks good. Her pregnancy is confirmed. My raw emotional reaction was happiness. I'm so thankful for that. But at the same time, the thought crossed my mind that maybe I won't have kids of my own. Not because I'll have the opportunity and actively choose not to, but because maybe it just isn't in the cards for me. And right now, I'm oddly okay with that. I will love my nieces and nephews with every bit of my heart. And I will be a part of their lives as much as humanly possible.

In this moment, I finally feel like what I have right now is enough. I don't feel like I'm missing anything. Which is odd, considering I'm technically missing several things people would expect me to miss—namely, a boyfriend, fiancé, or husband, and a baby. But I'm good right now. I feel happy for the first time in a long time. Maybe I have everything I need in life.

Tony Robbins says that, as humans, we have six core needs in order to feel motivated and fulfilled.

The first four, he says, are needs of the personality:

Certainty—the need for comfort, security, consistency, order, stability, etc. *Got that. I have a home, steady income, and a lot of routines.*

Uncertainty—the need for variety, excitement, adventure, and surprise. This one helps balance out the need for certainty because otherwise we would get bored. *I could maybe use a little more of this, but I'm working on it… maybe it's time to book that trip to Africa.*

Significance—the need to have meaning, a sense of importance, worth, being needed, etc. *I definitely have this at work. In my personal life? Hhmmmm… I think I do…?*

Love and Connection—the need for connection, attachment, love, and to be loved. *(sigh) I definitely have this with my family and friends. Do I have some work to do in the men arena? Yea, I guess I do.*

The final two are needs of the spirit:

Growth—the need for emotional, intellectual, and spiritual development. *Oh, I'm all over growth. Spiritual… hmmmm, religion kinda makes me uncomfortable.*

Contribution—the need to give, care, serve others, etc. *My new career goal should accomplish this.*

So from that perspective, I'm doing pretty well. Now, could one argue that romantic love is a necessary component of the Love and Connection need? Sure. But one could also argue that it isn't. TBD I guess.

These needs are a slightly different take on Maslow's hierarchy of needs, which I learned about in my undergrad psychology classes. But when you really compare them, you've got the same basic concept. We are here for an incredible experience. A human experience. It's really all about our connection with ourselves and our connections with others. We are meant to truly love, to make a difference, to really connect with each other, to challenge ourselves, to get out of our comfort zones, to grow—all the things I've been realizing over this past month.

Life is so much bigger than how I was living it. It's so much more than whether or not someone texted you back in an appropriate timeframe, keeping up with all the shows people are watching, dulling feelings with vodka, and even all the drama in the news. Why is it so clear now and it never was before? Why was I happy living my life until, slowly, I just wasn't? What is it inside of me that bubbled up to the surface?

I guess it's my third head. My true self.

Hadley's dad did say that most people don't even become aware of their third head until their late 20s or early 30s—that explains the poems I found from ten years ago. My third head wanted to be seen then, but I just ignored it and continued to live in my first and second head until ten years later. Until it "reared its ugly head" again. Only difference is, this time it won't be ignored. This time it's talking louder than the other two heads.

JOURNAL ENTRY: in the same day, *part 1*

MARCH 2017

As I've mentioned before, I have a history of making fun of *The Secret* and in no way believing in "that stuff." To this day, I've never read or seen *The Secret*, but I know its basic premise is that what you put out into the universe somehow affects what comes back to you. Well, I'm not great at admitting I'm wrong, but today I have a newfound belief and respect for "that stuff."

I agreed to run a local 15k with my friend Hadley. It's a big community event with some 10,000 runners. Early into the run, we came up to a woman with short dark hair who was running by herself. There was nothing about her that would stand out to anyone but me... but I knew immediately who she was. I hadn't seen her in many years, and those years had taken their toll ever so slightly, but I could have recognized her anywhere—she was first love Lloyd's mother.

Since I moved back home, I've wondered when I'll run into him... and Danielle... and their toddler son... and baby daughter. The day hasn't come yet, but I've played it out in my head a couple of times— in that daydream, I'm genuinely excited to see him and happy to meet Danielle. The kind of genuine kindness that would immediately dispel her likely assumption that I'm someone she would dislike. I'm determined to prove her wrong on that. His children are adorable, and I say "Hi" to them before telling him I'm so happy for him and walking away, likely leaving him a little shocked at how well that went. And when I play that out in my head, I'm of course wearing a super-cute outfit that day.

We caught up to Lloyd's mother and I lightly touched her arm to say hello. She smiled her kind smile as big as it could get and pulled me in for a mid-run hug. She kissed my cheek several times, telling me how good it was to see me. I was a little caught off guard by her level of emotion in that interaction. I immediately thought back to many years ago when I ran into her and she hugged me and whispered in my ear, "It took us a long time to get over you." *No kidding*, I replied in my head, *I'm still trying to get over your son.*

We had a brief exchange—she asked how I was doing and how I liked being an aunt. I answered her questions then said goodbye and ran on. I wondered for a second how she knew I was an aunt and laughed at the thought of one of Lloyd's sisters updating her on my life. Oh, Facebook. As I ran, I realized Lloyd and his family were likely on the course cheering her on. I quickly revised my daydream and played out a new version in my head where I see them on the side of the road, stop to say hello, and then the same scenario described above unfolds exactly as planned. Except I run away instead of walk away... and I'm not in a cute outfit—I'm sweaty.

Several miles later, I started to get hot and a little tired, and was distracted from being on Lloyd alert. And then, wouldn't ya know it, as soon as I stopped thinking about it... casually glancing around at the people out cheering on the runners... BAM—there he is. Lloyd. My first love.

He was smiling, holding his baby daughter on his hip, bouncing to the music while looking out for Grandma. A man version of the boy I was once so in love with. He looked the same to me. Just like when I look in the mirror I think I look the same. Neither are true.

I had a split second to decide whether or not to cut across the course to say hi to him and live out the daydream I've been preparing myself for the past three years.

I hesitated, and the second was gone. Mid-breath I told Hadley, "We just ran by my first love." She asked if I wanted to turn around to go back. I thought about it but decided not to. Instead, I ran on... maybe finally putting him behind me... as I've been trying to do for 16 years.

Plus... it's Lent. And that means no men.

So back to my beginning comment about what you put out into the universe affecting what it gives back to you... I'm halfway through my Lenten promise to give up men and I see Lloyd?? One of the men who has had the biggest impact on me... who I've had two and half years to run into and haven't. Are you kidding me? Why? Maybe to force me to face it. Maybe this is some kind of life test where I have to decide to run back to him or decide to run on. If that's the case, I'm legitimately happy I chose to run on.

But that's only half of it...

After the run, Hadley and I hung out at the post-race festivities for a few minutes and then decided to head back to our side of town for a much-deserved lunch. We were sitting there, eating and chatting about the run when my phone dinged for a text message. I glanced over and my jaw dropped at what I saw in the little text alert bubble.

"Oh... my... God," I said with a slight gasp.

Hadley looked at me confused, "Oh no—what?"

"I can't believe it," I said, now laughing. *Yes, I can believe it. I knew this day would come.* "It's Shane."

Her face immediately turned angry and, without hesitation, she said, "Don't respond."

Her reaction is understandable...

LOOKING BACK: dream guy

turned recurring nightmare

2014-2017

AGE: 30-32

May 2014

Shane and I fell in love very quickly. I had just
turned 30 and was still living in Ft. Lauderdale.
We were introduced through a mutual friend at
a Jaguars football game one weekend when I was
home visiting. That was a very brief encounter, but
eventually we started texting and that quickly turned
into wanting to get to know each other more, which
meant someone visiting the other. He came to see
me in South Florida and I remember sitting out on
my porch talking and laughing and feeling almost
uncomfortable with how immediately connected I

felt to him. We were connected on some level that I couldn't understand since we had basically just met. He was everything I always wanted—quick-witted, determined, a deep thinker, fun, family oriented... the list goes on and on. Icing on the cake? I'm not sure I've ever been more physically attracted to a man. I mean, look him up and down and have to take a deep breath kind of attracted. We maybe spent three weekends together and I knew I was in love. In fact, the first day of that first weekend, I texted my mother and sister, "There's zero chance I don't fall in love with this man." I just knew.

It was an inconvenient time for me to fall in love with someone who lived in a different city. I had just bought a condo and I was in the middle of my MBA program. Before meeting him, I had no plans of leaving South Florida. But I changed those plans very quickly.

Our fast love had me planning our future together after only a month of us being together. Knowing where the relationship was likely going, I decided it would be smart to start making some work contacts in Jacksonville. I would need people to reach out to the following year when I finished grad school and would be ready to move back home to be with Shane. What I wasn't expecting was for the first contact I made to have a job opportunity that was exactly what I wanted to do, and it was available right then. My MBA program was a remote weekend program so I could easily transfer to the program that met in Gainesville instead, which was only two hours from Jacksonville. And sure, I owned a condo, but whatever—I would just sell it. Maybe make some money. Before I knew it, I'd given notice to my job, listed my condo for sale, transferred MBA programs, and signed a lease for an apartment in Jacksonville. It all happened so fast and to be honest, I don't remember ever giving it a whole lot of thought. It all felt very *this is supposed to happen.*

My family was thrilled that I was moving back, but my South Florida friends (namely, Amber and Taylor) were of course worried I was making a rash decision for a man I didn't really know. And they were right. But I think on some level I also knew I needed to get out of South Florida. It had lost its luster for me.

When I first moved there, I was fresh out of college and still in full party mode—the be-out and be-seen lifestyle worked for me then. But over time, my hangovers got longer and my priorities began to shift. I couldn't keep up with the bar-beach-bar pace I lived in my early to mid-twenties. I was tired. And I was losing patience with the superficiality of it all. I've never been good at keeping up with latest fashion trend... or even caring about it. I'm an attractive person, but I never felt that way there, inside or out. Put me next to a skinny girl with boobs who knows how to do her hair and makeup and I don't get a second look. Plus, all the memories of the shameful mistakes I had made haunted me—driving by restaurants I'd gone to with Arlo, or Charlie's office building where we would meet super early in the morning to have sex before work. I needed to get away from all of it.

In the beginning of our relationship, Shane was affectionate, unguarded, all-in, extremely sweet, and open with his feelings. He would lean down to kiss me on the shoulder while I was blowdrying my hair. Walking down the street, he would lightly put his hand on my waist to guide me to the other side of him so he was walking closer to traffic. He cooked me dinner.

I fit perfectly in his arms.

August 2014

I first noticed the "shift" in our relationship three months into it, leading up to the weekend when he came down to move me. The plan I came up with was for him and a friend to drive down on Friday; we would load everything up in the U-Haul on Saturday morning, then head to the beach with my friends for one last beach Saturday like in the old days. On Sunday, we would wake up and drive north. Those plans changed when Shane's friend who was supposed to come down to help with the move bailed, so he had to find another friend to come help. But that friend couldn't stay until Sunday because he had to work. So Shane changed the plans to them driving down Friday night, packing up the U-Haul, and driving back to Jacksonville on Saturday, forgoing beach day.

In Shane's logical mind, it made complete sense and he was still helping me move so the change was no big deal. In my emotional mind, it was a big deal. I was so disappointed. And my friends, with the best of intentions, fueled the fire by insisting that he should find a way to stay on Saturday because it was important to me. Looking back on it, I can't help but laugh that I got so upset over going to the beach. It was all fine. He was still coming down to help me move *and* had convinced a friend who I had never even met to help. So that friend had to work. It really was no big deal.

But I see now the bigger issues at play—communication

and emotion vs. logic. These are without a doubt the two things Shane and I have struggled with over the years. He buries his emotion under logic. I'm equal parts logic and emotion, and the two are in a constant battle. I didn't logically communicate why the day was important to me—him getting to know the people who were important in my life, the people I was leaving for him. And he didn't emotionally acknowledge or understand why I was upset. Were either of us necessarily wrong? No. But could we have both done a better job communicating? Absolutely.

Unfortunately, my emotions were winning the battle in this instance—I wanted what I wanted so badly that I couldn't see through to the logic. And that is the moment I would say I lost my footing. I begrudgingly accepted the new plan of him leaving Saturday morning while I ran off to my farewell beach day, but at the same time, a seed was planted... a pesky little seed that I think every woman has dealt with at some point... one that would fester and grow and constantly convince me that something was owed to me—a seed I like to call "needy."

The beach day ended up being the perfect drunken send-off, and the next morning I drove to Jacksonville to start my new job and my new life with my now non-long-distance relationship. I still felt very positive about everything—I was going to love my job and Shane and I were going to live happily ever after.

Not exactly what happened.

October 2014

The best way I can describe the demise of my and Shane's relationship is the perfect storm. I've never dealt well with change. Just ask my siblings who roll their eyes every time I insist my parents read us *The Polar Express* and *The Night Before Christmas* on Christmas Eve even as adults—because that's our tradition. Throughout my eight years living in South Florida, I probably changed apartments six times, and every time I moved it threw me off emotionally.

In this case, I had just moved from the life, routine, and friends I had known for the past eight years to a new job and a new apartment in a new city where I would have to make new friends. All the change left me feeling very insecure and vulnerable. Thankfully, we were smart enough not to move in together after only a couple months of dating, so I had my own apartment. But with no new friends yet, that equated to a lot of alone time. I wanted—and felt like I needed—to lean on Shane to help me through all the change. He, on the other hand, had just started his own business and was all-in on making it work for a lot of reasons I didn't take the time or interest to fully understand. It all resulted in me being extremely needy and him being extremely busy. Not a good combination.

We did have good times, but it wasn't like the beginning. It felt different. I knew it and I'm sure he did too. But neither of us wanted to acknowledge it. It was in all the silent moments where you could see the most change—he didn't find little reasons to touch me as he walked by. I started playing those stupid games girls play where we hint that we're upset, hoping to get some attention. Every time I did something with the intent of getting him to open back up, I got the opposite from him. And the more he closed himself off, the more needy I got.

I would try to talk to him about "us" but I always approached it from the direction of what I needed but wasn't getting. He would respond with what I wanted to hear, but with no emotion behind his words. I remember one time, as we were laying on the couch, saying to him, "I need you to make me happy like you used to." He responded that everything he was doing was for us. Very sweet answer. But the fact that it had been said with zero emotion made it no answer at all to me.

But still, what a terrible thing for me to say! When I think back on those times, I almost don't recognize myself.

It's like I had reverted back to the needy teenage Kacie who was too young to handle her feelings. I had let my life and happiness once again revolve around a man. And the worst part is that I was completely unaware of it. I remember a conversation with my mother where I told her that I wasn't sure if it was going to work out between Shane and me because I didn't think he could give me the emotional support that I needed. I told her I was going to see how the holidays went and then make a decision in the New Year. What I didn't tell her was that my secret plan was that if I did break up with him, it would make him realize how much he loved me, we would get back together, and he would go back to being the affectionate, sweet, all-in, unguarded, and open with his feelings person I had first fallen in love with.

Oh the games we play.

November 2014

Well we didn't even make it through the holidays. I spent Thanksgiving with my family up in Charlotte, where my sister lived at the time, and had plans to fly back the Friday after Thanksgiving to be home for his birthday that Sunday. Literally on my way to the airport, I got a text from him that said, "I got my first birthday present" with a picture of tickets to the Florida vs. Florida State game on Saturday. The game was in Tallahassee. I immediately called him. He answered and told me that his friend had bought him tickets and they were going to drive over Saturday morning and stay the night.

I flipped out. "I'm on my way to the airport to fly home to be with you on your birthday and now you're leaving to go to the game?? I'm leaving my family to be with you!"

He argued that his best friend had just surprised him with tickets—what was he supposed to do?

The conversation is a blur at this point, but I know it ended abruptly. I ran into the airport, changed my flight, and stayed the rest of the weekend in Charlotte with my family. I texted him later, saying for him to call me when he could because, "We need to talk."

No call that night.

No call on Saturday.

When my flight landed back in Jacksonville on Sunday and I turned on my phone, there was no voicemail, no text. On my drive home from the airport, I decided to be the bigger person and I called him. He didn't pick up—I left him a voicemail saying that we clearly needed to talk but I still wanted to wish him a happy birthday. He ended up texting me later that day, thanking me for the birthday wishes. I responded again that we needed to talk, and he agreed, but didn't want to do it on his birthday. The next day, I called and left a message, trying to arrange this conversation we needed to have.

Nothing.

A few days later, I called and left another message, saying that this was the last message I was leaving and that I couldn't believe that, after everything, he wasn't going to at least call me back and have an adult conversation.

Nothing.

Like most people in my life while all this was happening, you're probably in shock that he just never responded. I was too. But this is something I've learned about Shane—when he doesn't know how to deal with something, or doesn't want to deal with something, he just doesn't deal with it. I'm not making excuses for him. That's just fact.

December 2014

I, on the other hand, and as evidenced by the Lloyd story, always want closure. So reverting back to my first love dramatic flair days, I wrote Shane a closure letter around Christmas.

The letter took the stance of understanding instead of anger. I acknowledged my part in the demise of our relationship and told him I had no hard feelings toward him. I explained how hard it was to understand why he wouldn't talk to me, but that still I meant it when I said I would always love him.

The difference with this closure letter was that I did get a response. I woke up one morning a week or so later to a long text from him, thanking me for the letter and saying I'd done nothing wrong in the relationship. He confessed to pushing me away because of his own issues. He said he would always love me.

I didn't know what to do or how to feel. I was still so hurt and confused, yet so happy to hear from him. Though we were only together for about seven months (only four of them in the same city), I missed him. I'd be lying if I said my mind hadn't occasionally wandered into thinking he had met someone else. Those are dangerous, painful roads to let your mind go down. I felt so relieved that wasn't the case.

2015-2016

Over the next five or six months, we went back and forth between communicating consistently and not at all. Every now and then, we would get together... usually when one of us had been drinking. Sometimes we would have good, honest conversations about what had happened and how we felt. I was always hoping it would be the start of us getting back together, but it never was. He was really busy and focused on his business, and blah, blah, blah. I would say I understood, but I really didn't. All I understood was what I wanted, and I wanted for us to be together. When I didn't hear from him on my birthday in May that year, I pulled the plug on everything. I told him I couldn't do it anymore and that he needed to stop contacting me. He did.

And then that whole scenario pretty much went on

repeat for the next year and a half. Something would trigger the communication—usually a drunken outreach by him. We would then start texting... and then start occasionally sleeping together... and then he would not follow through on some promise of getting together and I would tell him not to contact me anymore.

One time, after we hadn't spoken in months, he drunkenly called to say he was going to drive down to Gainesville where I was in class for my MBA program because he needed to see me that badly. I told him "no" and to call me the next day and we could arrange to talk. He never called.

Throughout all of this back and forth, I dated here and there and I know he did too. One time, I unblocked him on Facebook out of curiosity. He's never been a Facebook person—he has an account but does nothing with it. I pulled up his page and almost threw up when a bunch of pictures of him and some girl popped up. She was clearly an over-Facebooker and had tagged him in like seven pictures from the same night. Pictures where she was sitting on his lap. Pictures where his arm was around her. Pictures where he was kissing her cheek. I started to shake— the same freezing, shaking insides as when Samantha first called me to ask about the text messages between me and Arlo. It must be some kind of emotional overload that my body can't physically handle.

September 2016

The most recent disappearing act was just as bad as the first. I had just broken up with Adam, and Shane and I decided to start dating again. Emphasis on the word 'dating.' We agreed we didn't want to jump back into a relationship and we acknowledged our tendency to make things all about sex. So in an attempt to go about things the right way this time, we decided not to have sex until we had been on like ten dates.

It was going well, but admittedly not great. We were having good conversations but not great ones. I could tell he was still very guarded, and I couldn't help but desperately want him to open up, despite all of my attempts to stay strong and independent.

December 2016

It was over this past Christmas when he disappeared again. This time with even less explanation. We hadn't gotten into a fight. As far as I knew, everything was fine. We talked about hanging out before I left for D.C. to spend Christmas at my sister's, and I reached out to him that day but never heard back. I reached out to him a couple of days later and, again, got nothing. I got worried and called him and left him a message, saying I was worried and to please call me back... nothing. On Christmas day, I wished him Merry Christmas.... nothing.

Cue the feelings of apathy.

A day or so before New Year's Eve, I sent him a long, angry text calling him a coward for pushing me away again—assuming that either he didn't love me and just didn't have the balls to tell me, or he did and he was just scared. Either way, I was done and told him it was the last communication he would ever get from me.

January 2017

Uggghhh. So this is difficult to admit and I'm not proud of it—but even after that text where I so strongly said it was the last he would hear from me, I was still worried about him. There was a part of me that just couldn't accept that he would disappear like that. I legit worried that maybe something had happened to him. I thought about driving by his place to see if his car was there. But just because his car was there wouldn't mean he was okay. I would have to drive by *again* a day or so later to see if it had moved. Now that's just getting ridiculous. I couldn't bring myself to be "that girl."

Although, I did laugh at the thought of me driving slowly by with a hat pulled down low and wearing those glasses with a mustache attached to them.

Thankfully I didn't do that. But I did text him a month or so later, saying that I was legit worried about him and just wanted to know if he was physically okay. And wouldn't ya know it, he responded to that—he said he was okay and hoped I was as well. I remember feeling this strange combination of happiness and relief that he was okay, but devastation at what that meant. It meant he really had chosen to cut me out of his life with no explanation. It meant that maybe he stopped loving me.

Reliving and writing out this story is a total mindfuck by the way. It calls out a big internal conflict between how the situation appears and how I feel about it. I know how easy it is to paint him as the bad guy, but he's not what you're imagining. He's complicated. As I am, I guess. Behind his guard, he is unbelievably sweet and selfless and thoughtful. He has insecurities although he'll never admit it, and he is extremely hard on himself. He doesn't see himself like I see him. I see him for the man who I know he truly is—the man behind the guard. The one who was so open and loving. I still love him to this day, despite everything. People have a really hard time understanding that, especially my close friends and family. And it's difficult to explain. I guess I've just always seen him for the man who he truly is... never the man who he currently was—the one with the magical disappearing act. (eye roll)

I often feel bad for the people in my life who've had to watch me stumble through all of this, all the while listening to me defend every trip and fall. For my family and friends reading this—I'm sorry. I know it's hard to watch me keep going back to this man who's continuously caused me pain for the last three years. But for whatever reason, I've just never felt over him. The only way I can think to explain it is with an analogy...

It's like I'm walking down a long hall carrying a really heavy bag. And I'm struggling. Everyone around me just wants me to put the bag down. They yell to me that I don't need it... or it's too heavy... or it's not the right bag for me. Some people try to pry the bag out of my hands. But I love the bag. It's mine and I don't want to lose it. No one can convince me otherwise.

What I need everyone to understand is that it's *my* bag to carry. And I have to be the one who decides when to put it down. If I drop it too early, or if it's taken out of my hands, I may keep walking but I'll always be looking back at it, wondering if it's still there or if someone else picked it up. But when I decide I've carried it far enough, when I don't want it anymore, I will place it down gently (okay, maybe not so gently) and walk on... never looking back.

And rather than yell at me to drop it or try to take it from me, all I've ever wanted was for those around me to just walk along beside me, every so often checking in and asking if I'm okay.

JOURNAL ENTRY: in the same day, *part 2*

MARCH 2017

I unlocked my phone to read the text message and I legit could not believe what it said…

Shane

What's that sound app that helps you sleep?

Several reactions flooded my mind at once.

Confusion: Huh?

Anger: Are you f-ing kidding me? After what you did to me, you're going to randomly text me asking about an app?

Frustration: Why are you asking *me*? There are a million white noise apps. Google it!

Humor: You can't make this stuff up.

Relief: Yaaaayyyy, you still love me. (I'm not proud of that one.)

"I'm not responding," I said and put my phone back down. I went back to eating my sandwich, every now and then pausing to chuckle or sigh about the situation. I just kept asking Hadley, "Was that for real?"

She was in shock too. And it's a twofold shock: first, that after his most recent disappearing act, he would resurface at all, let alone to ask about a sleep app three months later; and second, that I hear from him on the same day I just saw Lloyd for the first time in like ten years. All when I'm trying to avoid men! The two I've loved the most pop up in my universe on the same freaking day.

After lunch, I went home and took a nap. I woke up to another text message from him...

Shane

Sorry to bother you.

Home alone with no one to convince me not to, I responded to him...

I won't chit chat with you. But if you want to have a conversation about what happened between us, I would be open to that.

He replied that that was a good idea and asked what my schedule was like that week. While part of me wanted to have the conversation as soon as possible, I decided to stick to my Lenten plan and told him that I couldn't do it until after Easter, so to contact me then. I laughed a little to myself, as I was sure that response made zero sense to him.

He (of course) asked why it had to be after Easter and I told him it was none of his business. I purposefully kept my responses short and quickly ended the conversation.

I knew my strength to stick to my Lenten promise only went so far with him. If there was a man out there who would be my kryptonite, it was him. Hands down. He's the one I've been waiting for… my dream guy… everything I wanted… until he didn't want me. And every time he's changed his mind and wanted me back, even if only for a night, I've jumped at the opportunity.

I'm not sure I've ever really said no to him. In three years, I think I've said yes to every opportunity to hang out with him, no matter what plans it meant cancelling. (face palm)

My emotions are confused. There's a little bit of happiness that I heard from him, a little bit of fear over the idea of falling back into another scenario where I end up hurt, and mostly annoyance because it's a big distraction from my quest to figure out my life.

I probably won't even hear from him after Easter. And with that thought I've forced him out of my mind and am refocused on me.

Perhaps it was another test from the universe—jump at the chance to reconnect with Shane like I always have or put myself first. If that's the case, I'm again proud of my decision.

I'm two for two.

JOURNAL ENTRY: a come-to-Jesus

MARCH 2017

Okay, I'm starting to feel even *more* connected to the universe... or is it God?

I hesitate to use the term God because I struggle with it and all the preconceived notions attached to that word/name. I was raised Catholic, going to church just about every Sunday and Catholic school all the way through high school. At an early age though, I questioned the man-made part of organized religion. My dad's mother—the grandmother who gave me the stamp collection—was Lutheran and about once a month, we would go to church with her. I liked her church better because it was smaller, we always sat in the same row, and everyone knew my grandmother and said hello. For communion, we got to go up on the altar and kneel on this long, velvet kneeler while someone brought us the host and tiny plastic cups of wine on pretty gold and glass trays. I thought that was more fun than the way we did it at our Catholic church. Remember, I was a kid.

One day in the car after church, I asked my grandmother, "What's the difference between Catholics and Lutherans?" She told me the story of how Martin Luther separated from the Catholic Church because of reasons I can't remember right now and started his own religion. I remember thinking *hmmmm, he just got to start his own religion?* Even at a young age, I knew that just didn't quite add up. How can someone just start their own religion if religion is based on what God told us he wants? Or at least, that's what I was learning in my Catholic elementary school.

My issues with organized religion can perhaps be traced back to that conversation. Someone doesn't agree with an aspect of a religion so they just go off and create another one. And how many other religions were formed that way? *A lot.* It didn't make sense to me as a child and I certainly don't agree with it now that I'm an adult.

Many years ago, I made some sense of organized religion in my head—religion is humankind's interpretation of something that is bigger than us, something we can never truly comprehend. And I say that for all religions because to me, despite some of their significant differences, they are all based on the same principal—that there is something bigger than us, something more.

(To be completely honest... the first time I came to that conclusion was during a very late-night, post-bar, cocaine-induced conversation with a friend. We started trying to answer one question... if God created the universe, what was there before that? And what was God doing before that? Just hanging out? It's a pretty impossible question to answer, and I think that's because our minds might not be capable of fully understanding the concept of God. And for the record, I don't do any drugs now, but I do applaud their ability to take your mind into places your sober mind restricts you from.)

A good analogy here is different languages—why are there different languages? Because human beings in different parts of the world created their own way of communicating, their own way of describing the world around them. Everyone is still having the same conversations about the same objects, same feelings, same thoughts, etc. The communication—or the way people are describing those things—is the only difference. Same for different religions—human beings in different parts of the world created their own way of describing, interpreting, and paying homage to something bigger than they could fully understand, something more. No one is wrong or right—people just speak different religious languages.

Even as I realized this though, I still struggled to find my relationship (my description and interpretation) with this "Something More." As an adult, I do not go to church. And at this point in my life I rarely, if ever, pray. When I was in my early teens, I remember not being able to fall asleep until I prayed. I don't know if it was strong faith or just habit, but I was convinced I could not go to sleep until I prayed. Somewhere along the way I lost that faith, or at least that habit.

I did go to church a couple of times in college... it was actually during the prime of my party days. I always went alone and I don't think I told any of my friends where I was going. I'm not really sure what inspired me to go—maybe I was starting to feel a little lost and was looking for something. Whatever it was, going to church wasn't the answer because I didn't go more than a handful of times. And during the years after college, I would sometimes think about how I didn't pray anymore, and I would wonder why. I would even start to try again but it never stuck. Sometimes I felt like I was faking it and that God could tell, and that was even worse than not praying at all (gotta love Catholic guilt).

A couple of years ago, I started reading the book *Proof of Heaven*. It's a neurosurgeon's account of a near death experience he had. I enjoyed the book even though I didn't finish it. I think I stopped reading it because I got what I wanted out of it about halfway through. What I took away from that book was the author's description of God, or Ohm, as he referred to him (because he said that's the best way he could describe the sound when you are near him/it). He said that Ohm has more human characteristics than we would ever imagine—things like humor and irony. There was something about that thought that gave me so much peace. To think that God wasn't this almighty Being sitting up in Heaven and judging me for my choices, feeling disappointed in me for not living up to my potential. Instead, to think of him as human-like, as someone who maybe chuckled as he watched me stumble through life. I liked that.

After reading that book, I started praying again but I took a different approach. I didn't start with all the "Dear God" formalities; I didn't say any Hail Marys or Our Fathers; I just talked. I talked to him like I would a friend—talking about what I was worried about, including worries about what he thought about my new praying style. I was just honest. That lasted for a while, but it didn't stick either. I couldn't tell you why.

Not long ago, I randomly stumbled across a YouTube video of an interview with a 13-year-old genius physicist. He was being interviewed about some energy device he invented to help with the world's energy crisis. The interviewer asked him, "What is God?" He answered that God is energy, describing the idea that he is an energy form that created all, is in all, and *is* all. He then went on to say that the Bible actually explains quantum physics laws and astrophysics experiments and theories. Now, I don't know about all that because I don't know the first thing about quantum physics or astrophysics, but the energy definition was very intriguing to me. At the time, I didn't give the video much thought after watching it and sending it to my brother, who is a self-proclaimed agnostic atheist.

(By the way, I promise I'm getting to why I feel more connected to the universe... or God... or energy... or Something More... or whatever...)

Back in January, I had a girls' weekend with my three best friends from South Florida—Amber (my old roommate), Taylor (who I went to college with), and Charlotte (who I met through Taylor). Before the weekend, I was shopping and came across some small prayer boxes. They were little tin boxes with tiny pieces of paper and a tiny pencil in them. They were just really cute. Inside the cover, each read, "When your head starts to worry, and your mind just can't rest, put your prayers down on paper, and let God do the rest." I decided to buy one for each of my friends—not that any of us are extremely religious, but we were all struggling with something in our lives, whether we were admitting the extent of it or not. I gave them each the prayer box mostly as a symbol that we were all dealing with things, big things, and we needed to rely on help (which we often didn't ask for) to get through it. It was also a subtle plea for them to stop worrying so much, as both Taylor and Charlotte struggle with anxiety. Originally, I wasn't going to buy myself a box because there were only three of the style I wanted to get them. But then I saw one with an elephant on it that said "be happy." I love elephants, so I couldn't resist and bought it for myself.

When I got home from the girls' weekend, I was feeling really down. Like I didn't want to be home. I didn't want to go back to my everyday life. We had such a fun weekend just drinking and talking—we literally never left the beach condo where we were staying. I had what we'd coined "post weekend depression"—a common feeling after fun, alcohol-tastic weekends. The night I got home, before I went to bed, I wrote "I pray to always cherish time with my friends."

I started to write in it each night. My first couple were similar to my old prayer habit, where I started with *"I pray for..."* and then wrote something big-picture. After a few nights of that, for some reason I switched to just writing what was on my mind. Either a statement or a question or a request... *"give me strength" "what should I do" "thank you."*

And this is where it starts to get weird—recently, I've started to notice answers to those questions or responses to those requests or statements. No joke. Not always right away, but they're coming.

The night I found the poems, before I turned off my light to go to sleep, I wrote "I need to write" on the tiny piece of paper. And now I'm writing this book.

A couple of days before the race where I saw Lloyd and heard from Shane, I was driving home from work and I had the urge to reach out to Shane and ask to meet for coffee. I wanted to try to understand why he disappeared, but mostly I wanted to tell him that I now understand the life changes he was going through when we first got together—the desire to change your path and the focus and determination it takes to do that. Not that it excuses him for how he treated me, but I wanted him to know that I understood it more now than I had before. I thought that might give me peace. I wrote in my prayer box that night, "Should I?" And then I heard from him a couple of days later.

I mean, I guess you could argue coincidence but you have to admit it's a little strange.

Today is Sunday and I went in to work for a couple of hours. On my way home, my mind started doubting if I would really be able to accomplish all these goals I've been uncovering and writing down. *What am I doing? Who am I to write a book?* I was feeling tired. I knew I should go home and either read or write, but part of me just wanted to lay on the couch and watch TV.

I got home and put some motivational videos on in the background as I began to make my lunches for the week. They got me thinking about my goals and I randomly remembered that I had written some down a long time ago in the back of the book, *The Last Lecture*, which I read probably close to ten years ago. Now keep in mind that I haven't opened or even thought about that book in a long time. I found it on my book shelf, turned to the back page, and sure enough, there were the goals I had written:

To Do:

- Write a book
- Go to Africa
- Be on *The Today Show*
- Make a difference in an underdeveloped country
- Have a baby

More confirmation that this has always been in me. I've had these goals—or desires—for a long time, and I haven't been focused on them because I've been too busy worrying about my love life and my social life, and the lane my life was supposed to stay in according to everyone else.

(The "have a baby" one stings a little.)

There were two journals on the shelf next to the book. I figured they were empty because I didn't remember ever writing in them; I've never kept a journal (until now, I guess). I opened the first one to check. The first page was a note from the friend who gave it to me and the rest of the pages were blank. I opened the second one. It has elephants on the cover and I immediately remembered that Amber gave it to me for my birthday one year. All the pages were blank as well, except for the first one:

January 4th, 2016

A New Year.
Once again, I feel lost. Less lost than last year but still lost.
Maybe it is the decisions I have made—trying to decipher between who I am, who I'm meant to be and who I'm holding myself back from becoming.
Maybe it's loneliness.
The pendulum swings so quickly between feeling lost and feeling like I'm exactly where I'm supposed to be.
Where is the middle?

I wasn't even shocked by this one and I have zero recollection of writing it. This is the exact kick in the ass I needed—it's even more proof that I haven't been on track for a long time and that deep down I've known it. Seeing that reenergized me to keep writing this book and keep working on figuring out what I *really* want out of life. I didn't cry like when I found the other writings. I just felt connected to the universe... or God... or Ohm... or energy... or whatever you want to call it. It feels like the Something More is listening to me. And better yet, responding.

JOURNAL ENTRY: spiraling out

MARCH 2017

One of the videos I had playing a week or so ago mentioned a universal law of growth in nature. I was intrigued by that soundbite so I paused whatever I was doing and glanced at the TV—what I saw was an image of a spiral, almost looked like a seashell. The video didn't go into detail about it, but the overall concept stuck with me—the universal law of growth is a spiral.

This evening, I dug deeper into it. The video was referring to the Fibonacci spiral, which is based on the Fibonacci sequence. It's a sequence of numbers—0 1 1 2 3 5 8 13...—where the next number is always the sum of the previous two numbers. From the numbers, you get the golden rectangle, and then the golden mean creates a spiral, or something like that. That's the best I can explain it; I'm no mathematician.

However, the more I learned about it, the more I fell in love with it. It's growth—in nature, in humans, in animals. It's organic growth.

Seriously, the Fibonacci spiral/ratio is found in the growth patterns of a crazy amount of living things. If you don't believe me, Google it.

The spiral starts out in a tight pattern but as it continues, the spaces between the lines (or the overall size) become larger. It's hard to put into words why I find that so meaningful to me right now. Obviously I relate it to what I now want to call a "growth spurt" instead of an existential crisis. It shows how big change and significant growth happen slowly and incrementally, so quietly at first that you don't know they're happening. Then the growth reaches a point of being uncomfortable, like the outer edges of the spiral are stretching you outside of your comfort zone. When you become aware of it and commit to it, the growth goes from being incremental to exponential. (Like how I got all math-y there?)

What I love most about it is that it starts from zero. When you think about it in terms of personal growth or any type of change we want to make in our lives, we are zero. We are all we need to grow. We just need to take that first step—1. And then another step—1. And then with each step, the next step (and subsequently the sum total) becomes bigger and bigger. I think too often we look at an end result— the distance from the starting point of the spiral to the outermost line—and think we can't do it; we can't make whatever change it is that we want; we can't achieve what we want; we can't have the life we dream about. Because it will be too difficult—it seems like such a stretch.

But we don't go from 0 to 55 all at once so we shouldn't look at it that way. According to Fibonacci, we go from 0 to 1; and then from 1 to 1; then 1 to 2, 2 to 3, 3 to 5, etc. Each step, while it remains only one step, creates more and more change. If we just look at the next step, instead of the end result, everything all of a sudden seems possible. I love that.

But there's another fascinating element to it. The spiral is found in almost everything... just like energy is in everything... just like maybe God, or Ohm, or Something More is in everything. So it makes sense that the Fibonacci spiral is sometimes referred to as "God's thumbprint."

For the record, my intention is not to make this book religious or spiritual in any way. I'm literally sitting in my bed typing this thought process as it comes to me. For so long, I've struggled with my faith and I think I've finally found something I believe. God (and I'm still uncomfortable using that term but I will for lack of a better one) is not as I was taught He was when I was growing up—this external, all-knowing Being watching all of us. God *is* us. Many religions say that God is in all of us. But again, that makes Him an external force. When you really switch the thinking to God *is* us, it changes everything. He—or I think I prefer saying 'It' because it removes the external Being who is for some reason almost always a masculine element—is the energy and the life force in everything. If you think about it, that concept explains everything from religion and *The Secret* to psychics, magic, and even witchcraft (confession: I love the movie *The Craft*). They are all different ways of explaining, witnessing, or tapping into the energy force that *is* everything.

That's a little mind-blowing to me.

And if it's true, organized religion did get one thing right—God is the creator of all things. What they left out was the preferred design aesthetic: a spiral.

JOURNAL ENTRY: big moves and 'Big' questions

MARCH 2017

Earlier this week I was thinking about the other goals on my list, other than writing this book. I technically have three lists I could choose from:

There's the goals list I wrote in the back of *The Last Lecture*:

- Write a book
- Go to Africa
- Be on *The Today Show (Maybe this book will accomplish that!)*
- Make a difference in an underdeveloped country
- Have a baby *(gulp)*

Or I have the list I found along with the poems that put me in tears. Those were separated out in one, three, and five-year goals:

1yr

- Healthiest I've ever been.
- Balance in my life—health, fun, friends, gym *(Well this has been a constant struggle.)*
- Career advancement
- Find out what inspires me *(Wow, I can't believe I wrote this as a goal back then.)*

3yr

- Financially stable
- Dating more *(Ugh, that one really backfired.)*
- Define my religious beliefs *(Another ironic wow.)*
- Write more

5yr

- Completely out of debt
- In committed/serious relationship
- Write a book

So the good news is I have actually completed some of these goals. Not necessarily in the timeframe spelled out above, but whatever. Year one and year three goals are either completed or in the process of being completed, aside from dating more—but that's dropped way down on the life priority list.

Then I also have the list I've made recently:

- Write a book—*Working on it!*

- Go to Africa

- Get and stay out of debt—*On my way to accomplishing this one too!*

- Start a company that helps children get out of poverty

- Get a graduate degree in either Psychology or Organizational Behavior—*Trying to satisfy one of my original goals that I strayed from, becoming a psychologist. I've added in Organizational Behavior as an option because I worry Psychology degrees are more science/research intensive than I want. Organizational Behavior might be a better route. I say that without really knowing what the degree entails—but I know I loved that class in my MBA program because it was all about studying people. That's my draw to Psychology—I love to learn how people think, why we feel the way we feel, etc. It's fascinating.*

If I look at these and come up with a master list and

a plan to achieve them, it looks something like this:

GOAL: Write a book

PLAN: Continue to journal every day during Lent. After Lent, go back through to clean up and fill in backstories. Then research editorial/publishing process. I only have a vague idea of how all that works.

GOAL: Get and stay out of debt

PLAN: Put together a comprehensive list of my current expenses and schedule a meeting with my financial advisor to come up with a budget and plan to pay off my credit card debt and save for...

GOAL: Go to Africa AND make a difference in an underdeveloped country. I think I can combine these two goals by going to Africa on a mission trip and attaching a mini vacation to that trip to go on a safari.

PLAN: Research mission trip options and the costs of including a safari. Figure out with my financial advisor how long it will take me to save enough money and then book the trip.

I'm holding out on the goals of starting my own company and getting another degree for now. They aren't financially possible... yet. And I'm not entirely sold on the starting my own company idea. I think it's what I want to do, but I don't *know*. Something just doesn't feel right yet.

A funny universe-talking-to-me story: I put on the motivational speeches while I ran this evening. If I heard a phrase or thought process that I liked or that got me thinking, I typed it into my phone notes app so I wouldn't forget. I can't remember what word I was typing, but it was a normal word and I did it so fast that I totally butchered whatever it was supposed to be, and it autocorrected to UNICEF. Now I know what UNICEF is because I looked into jobs there back when I was at the PR firm and didn't know what I wanted to do next. It was part of my "make a difference in an underdeveloped country" thought process. I've never typed UNICEF in my current phone (or in any cell phone, for that matter), so there's no way it's in the autocorrect history. It popped up this evening and that's when I had the idea that a mission trip to Africa could accomplish my goal of making a difference in an underdeveloped country. Thank you, universe (or Something More).

Another interesting tidbit about my run tonight... I was the only one out of the group who showed up. Usually David runs on the beach by himself if no one from the group shows up. I know he really enjoys that and secretly hopes for no-shows sometimes. Because it was just the two of us, we decided to run on the beach. We didn't talk—I listened to my phone and he ran in silence. But after I got home, we had a surprising text exchange:

David

Thanks for coming today!

Me

No—thank YOU for not cancelling. I know how important that quiet alone time is to you. I appreciate you letting me intrude.

David

You're one of like 3 people that understand me in this world hahaha so that means you're allowed in my quiet time

Me

Ditto

David

Actually the more I think about it probably just 2 people

You and my dad

Key person missing from that group. Every now and then, I find myself still questioning our relationship. Should it be more? Or are we just great friends? After we talked about what happened between us, I was asked by both Hadley and Rachel if I thought there was more there. My answer to them was that I've always discounted him as a romantic option, admittedly for reasons that aren't very valid. (1) he's much younger than me, which means we are at different stages in our lives in terms of what we want next. And, (2) his career is a mod-podge of different part-time jobs. The first reason has lost some of its weight since I've removed 'get married and have kids' off my necessity list and onto my 'it will be nice if it happens' list. And the second reason is just snobby and a product of years of living in a 'job snob' circle. Twice I've been in a serious relationship with men who didn't go to college—Arlo and Shane. It never bothered me. Arlo was a personal trainer in addition to a lab technician. He had an incredible work ethic that I admired immensely. And Shane is an entrepreneur who successfully started a very profitable small business. His work ethic amazed me. A common theme here—work ethic. David also has an incredible work ethic. I guess a work ethic is more important to me than any degree or job title. If given the chance, my parents would agree. But when I was dating Arlo and Shane, I always worried it bothered them. Maybe it did. Or maybe it didn't, and it's just another example of me caring too much about what I fear other people think instead of just focusing on what's important to me. Ugggghhhh.

Maybe I'm so attracted to people who have a work ethic because it's the trait I always wanted to have but was never able to find in myself until now. Maybe I seek out in men what I've so desperately wanted in myself but could never achieve because I was too afraid of what my circle would think. Which is silly because people respect people who work hard. But in my all-or-nothing nature, I didn't know how to be a hard-working party girl. Hence my constant search for balance I guess.

David and I do have a connection though. Just like Shane and I do. And I love them both. David I love for the person he is, the friend he is, and the role that he plays in my life. He's like a non-romantic soulmate. It almost feels like, in another life, David and I were brother and sister.

And in that other life, Shane and I were romantic soulmates. As a *Sex and the City* fan, I've joked that he's my Mr. Big. No matter what he does or how he hurts me, he always comes back, and I always let him. But

I fear that analogy isn't healthy because Carrie and Big end up together. And I don't want to think that Shane and I will. Because what if we don't? There's a saying that rejection creates obsession. Maybe it's just his rejection of me that makes me hold onto him.

JOURNAL ENTRY: it's starting to sink in

MARCH 2017

Recently, I watched a TED talk—*How To Make Stress Your Friend* by Kelly McGonigal. It's a very interesting topic because she talks about how stress is really only harmful if we think it's harmful. But if we instead view it as our body gearing up to tackle the challenge in front of us, the negative effects of stress are erased. Because stress itself isn't really the enemy we have made it to be. It is our *belief* that stress is harmful that is the real enemy. If you change your mind about stress, you can change your body's response to stress. Easier said than done of course.

But my favorite part of the video is the last point she makes—that when we are stressed, our body releases oxytocin. All I knew of oxytocin prior to this talk was that it gets released during sex and makes us feel emotionally connected to the person we're with.

And I think maybe it happens more in women? I heard that a long time ago and just took it for truth. I've thought about that potentially incorrect factoid throughout my life since realizing this odd pattern I see so often (and have fallen victim to myself)…

Girl sleeps with boy.

Girl daydreams about it being the beginning of a relationship with boy.

Boy doesn't contact girl.

Girl blames herself for the silence, thinking boy must have lost respect for her for sleeping with him so soon.

Girl then convinces herself that can't be the case, as she is different than other girls and he should know that.

Still nothing from boy.

Girl defends her actions and her right to express her sexuality, citing that it's not the 1950s.

Girl decides she doesn't want to be with boy anyway and justifies this with several logical reasons proving he's not for her.

Case closed.

Not exactly the healthiest of exercises. Why do we fall into that pattern? Are we really "crazy" as we are so often accused of being, or is it chemical? Does the oxytocin trick us into thinking we want to be with a particular boy when, in reality, we just wanted to get laid and then that damn hormone messed with our mind? If men can think that simply and non-emotionally, why can't we? Why do we get so attached? I'm the attachment queen. Clearly. Hello staying in bad relationships too long and my inability to get over Shane.

In the last couple minutes of the TED Talk, Kelly McGonigal says that oxytocin is actually a stress hormone that primes us to do things that strengthen relationships. *"Your stress response has a built-in mechanism for stress resilience, and that mechanism is human connection."*

Connection. Now that's much different than attachment. This part of the video was a little bit of a slap in the face for me because for a long time, I've been doing just the opposite. When I'm stressed out or hurt, I don't talk to my friends about it and I don't talk to my family about it. I don't connect with them. Instead I try to deal with it all myself. Or actually, I don't think I even deal with it. I just push it down, brush it away, and ignore it.

Case in point—earlier in the year, when I wasn't in a good place, no one really knew. I made a comment to my mother and a couple of close friends, but I didn't really explain it. Throughout all the Shane back-and-forth, I never really talked to anyone about it—what was happening and how I was feeling. I just avoided it. And if Kelly's thought process is right, I was denying myself what I really needed—connection.

That explains a mini breakdown I had a couple of months after Shane and I broke up the first time. I was laying in bed one night and I just started crying. The tears started small and slow at first, but then they got bigger and faster—pouring out of me—and I couldn't stop them. I got so worked up that my stomach started to clench and I thought I was going to throw up. I ran to the bathroom and dropped to my knees in front of the toilet, but I couldn't throw up. My stomach didn't stop clenching and the tears wouldn't stop coming—so there I was, hysterically crying and dry heaving over the toilet on the floor of my bathroom, alone and in the dark. It was like all the hurt and emotions I'd tried to avoid and bury down deep inside of me had reached a boiling point. Out they were coming, and I couldn't stop them.

When I finally calmed down enough to breathe normally, I did reach out for help. I called my mother.

My dad picked up the phone—they were already asleep—and I asked to talk to Mom. I'm sure the late call terrified them.

"Kacie?" she asked into the phone, half asleep and half concerned.

"Mom," I said, still choked up from the tears, "I'm sad." It's all I could manage to say.

"I know, honey," she answered, her voice perfectly mirroring my sadness. I could tell she was tearing up. "What can I do? Do you want me to come over?"

I know her sadness that night existed on two levels—empathy for her crying daughter, and utter despair that there was nothing she could do to make it all better.

Of course, I didn't let her come over. I just told her I would be okay and that I was going back to sleep. She argued back, not wanting to hang up when I was so upset. But I insisted. And I'm not sure we ever talked about that night again. I still wouldn't connect.

Why do I do that? Why do I avoid talking to those who are closest to me about my real feelings? Better yet, why do I avoid really confronting my true feelings? I have this consistent history of shutting people out from my true emotions. Including myself.

And I know I'm not the only one who does this. For example, I've known several people in unhappy marriages, yet they refuse to talk about it with their friends or family. Why do we do this? Is it embarrassment that our decisions were wrong? Who cares? What's worse—making a wrong decision and doing something to change the negative consequences that came from that wrong decision, or making a wrong decision and actively deciding to keep reliving it day in and day out? We all make mistakes. And we all get hurt. And when that happens, we should lean on the people closest to us. What's the point of having a support system if we are never really going to use it for support?

That's partly why writing all of this is such a big step for me. I try not to think too much about what I'm writing and how it sounds, and instead just write... all of my emotions and thoughts, as raw as possible. I'm confronting it all—so hopefully connecting with myself—and then I plan to share it, and hopefully connect with others.

My second head is freaking out, but my third head is nodding along with acceptance.

JOURNAL ENTRY: happy Friday

MARCH 2017

It's a little more than halfway through Lent and it's Friday. My mother texted me earlier asking what I was doing tonight. I replied that I'm not doing anything and that I'm going into work tomorrow. She responded with a joke about me becoming her and saying that all work and no play is no fun—with a sad face emoji. I sighed and replied that the most successful people on this planet got there by working hard. She responded with a funny little video of someone doing a Friday dance.

Facepalm.

It's an interesting feeling to suspect your parents think you're not cool. I know she's just worried about me and just wants me to be happy…. but I'm still not sure she understands what happiness is for me. And it's not her fault. One conversation won't erase 10+ years of me going out with friends and telling her funny stories about our drunken excursions. There's probably a part of her that thinks I'm having some kind of a breakdown and giving up. Again, not her fault because, while I told them a good bit about what I was going through, I didn't tell them the extent of it. I never do.

Mother, if you're reading this, then please know that in this moment, on this Friday night when I am home alone in bed writing and you are probably worrying about me, I am exactly what you always say you want for me—happy. And I acknowledge that I don't tell you everything I'm thinking and feeling, and I know that's what you desperately want. I'm so sorry for that. I just can't right now. One day I hope you'll understand. One day I hope I make up for it.

JOURNAL ENTRY: here comes the sun

MARCH 2017

I love the weekends because I get to watch the sunrise (which I'm sure you've figured out by now). One of the cons of working in construction is that the days start so early. I'm lucky if I catch a glimpse of the morning light when I get in my car to head to work. I used to love the weekends because I could stay out late, sleep in, and day drink. Oh, how things have changed!

As I stood on the beach watching the sunrise this morning, I started thinking about why I love it so much. Sunsets are beautiful too. Why am I so partial to the sunrise?

"It's the start of a new day" is the obvious answer. And considering I feel like my entire life is the start of a new day these days, that certainly makes sense. But it's deeper than that. Yes, it is the start of the new day.... but, more so, it was dark and now it is light. And the process of going from dark to light is slow but beautiful. The colors fade in and brighten so subtly that you don't realize how rich they are getting until they're there. The change is barely recognizable. But what's causing it isn't slow or subtle at all. Without notice, the top of the bright burning sun appears, and it rises up against the horizon so quickly. What seemed so visibly slow was actually moving so fast, just below the surface. And once the sun rises up past the horizon, it seemingly slows down again. All day, you know the sun is moving, but you can't appreciate the pace when looking at it. That only happens when it passes the horizon. There is something so poetic in that.

I think change in your life is the same way. Like the sun, it rises up inside of you. You slowly become aware of it, just as the colors of the sky subtly change. But once it nears the surface, once you become really aware of this change inside of you that wants to break the horizon, and you let it happen, it's quick and it's bright and it's brilliant. It's so bright and shocking that it's difficult for the people in your life to look at directly, to really see it. Not until it's fully above the horizon, until the change is complete, does it become just part of the normal day again—and fully accepted. But the process of moving across the horizon is the shock; and it's also the true beauty.

It was a long time ago when my desire to watch the sunrise first appeared. Since I was a kid, our family vacation was to go fishing in the Bahamas. We would rent a boat and a house on a small island that's completely removed from the big resorts and tourist attractions. In the early years, the houses didn't have TVs and Wi-Fi didn't exist—our free time was spent playing card games or charades.

Every day, we would wake up early and head out to fish. We would spend all day on our boat—and it wasn't a big boat, by any means. My dad and brother would usually be in the back and my mother, sister, and I on the bow. We mostly spent our days fishing, but sometimes we would come back in for lunch and find a remote beach to relax on for a while. Essentially, we really had nothing to do but talk to each other all day, every day, and all night. It was the best.

Even as the years went on, and as the rental houses started to have TVs, we would never turn them on. Our traditions stuck—we played cards and charades and danced around the kitchen. In more recent years, the houses had Wi-Fi and we caved a little—we monitored work emails and responded to text messages but only in the mornings and evenings when we were at the house. We still spent all day, every day, bouncing around on a small boat with nothing to do but talk to each other.

We used to take this trip every year. But as us three kids have become three adults, two of whom are married, one with a baby and the other with a baby on the way, these trips are no longer annual. I'm sure we'll go again but it will be different. Not bad different, just different. Just like it was different when we added sibling spouses to the mix. I'll always long for the days when it was just the five of us sitting around the poker table laughing because someone was once again borrowing money from the "bank," or being out on the water and my dad yelling those two exhilarating words—"FISH ON"—and we all knew our roles to play to get the fish in the boat.

We can't go back to those days, but I cherish those memories.

We always woke up early to head out fishing but never before the sunrise. As my brother and I got older and more into fishing, we would push to get out there earlier and earlier, with the goal to be the first boat on our dock to leave. On a trip several years ago, I remember thinking how cool it would be to see the sunrise from the boat. My birthday happened to fall during that trip and I tried to get the family to agree to be out on the boat for the sunrise, but that request was denied. My dad wasn't comfortable taking the boat out in the dark and I understood that. Plus, no one else quite had the burning desire that I did to get up *that* early. But I was able to convince them all to wake up and watch the sunrise from the deck of our house on my birthday. My mother was supportive but my siblings gave me a hard time about it. Not in a mean way—mostly joking. And no one would have expected that to bother me, as I was known for not only being able to take those kinds of joking jabs, but dish them right back out as well.

But that time, I remember not understanding why they couldn't just enjoy this one thing for me. Why it couldn't just be special for all of us. How many people get a chance to watch a sunrise from a house on a charming remote island in the Bahamas? And even if my family members took that for granted, why couldn't they just support the idea because it was special to me, without any comments from the peanut gallery? This was one of several times when I couldn't take the jokes; not because I was feeling particularly sensitive that day, but because I was feeling like an outsider. Like what I wanted was different from what my family wanted... and therefore wrong. I never let them see these feelings. I just felt a little sad inside.

Two years ago, not long after Shane and I broke up (for the first time), I'd often stop and watch the sunrise on my way to work in the morning. There were a couple of weeks where the timing was perfect. I loved it. I loved starting my day that way. Around that time, Shane and I had one of our "reunions" that always got me hoping it was the beginning of us getting back together (and I was always wrong)... I told him how I had been watching the sunrise and really enjoying it, and he also jokingly made fun of me, saying he had been watching the moon rise and really enjoying it. And again, I felt like I was different.

Soon after that, I stopped making an effort to watch the sunrise... until about a year ago. Right after I finished grad school and right around the time I registered for the marathon... which I now realize was right about the time I think I (unknowingly) started to change... I guess that's the time when my sun started to approach the horizon.

JOURNAL ENTRY: gulp

MARCH 2017

As I go through this growth spurt, or transformation, or self-actualization process, or whatever you want to call it, I find myself really wanting the people in my life to go through the same thing. I've been thinking a lot about my South Florida friends lately—Amber and Taylor, my best friends. We have matching tattoos that translate into "soul mates." I've been through so much with them. Actually, "so much" doesn't even do it justice.

Amber was my roommate for six years—we came home to each other every night. There was no hiding our moods or internalizing our experiences. We shared everything. In those six years, she supported me through finding out that first love Lloyd was engaged... and then married... and then a father; she watched my close relationship with my family deteriorate as I made relationship decisions they didn't agree with and I subsequently shut them out; she endured me shutting her out to some extent when she questioned who I was in my relationships. And on the flip side, I called out of work when her heart was broken so we could watch movies all day; I talked her through dating a married man, and watched the roller coaster of emotions when she found out she wasn't the only affair he was having; I listened to her cry on the phone when she called me to tell me she lost her job.

Amber and I practically spent the entirety of our twenties together.

And I've known Taylor even longer, as we met in college. We spent countless hours sitting outside the sorority house and talking about life. I sat with her crying, looking at a positive pregnancy test... which (thankfully) ended up being a false alarm. I helped coordinate airport pick-ups and post-funeral plans when her mother passed away; I was there when her father passed away. Amber and I were bridesmaids in her wedding.

The three of us have experienced every emotion together. We've found ways to laugh through hard times and we've kept each other above water no matter what's tried to drown us. When I moved back to Jacksonville, the hardest part was leaving them. They were my family in South Florida. We were like sisters.

So why am I so hesitant to talk to them about how I'm feeling and the changes I want to make in my life? Is it the same reason it's difficult to talk to my mother? Is it because I crave their approval and support, or is it because I know they'll be the toughest critics? I fear their rejection of the Kacie that doesn't want to go out to the bar or even just sit around and have a drink... which then turns into several... then into bottles and bottles of wine. To say our lives have revolved around drinking is a bit extreme, but to say our lives have been underlined by drinking is no stretch at all.

What do you want to drink?

When can we start drinking?

What's your drinking strategy?

I need a drink.

That has been the soundtrack of so much of our time together. How do I tell them I no longer want to sing that song?

I've started to tell Amber a little bit. She's the one who tried to get me to watch *The Secret* so many years ago. She was always a fan of self-help or self-improvement stuff, and I always gave her a hard time about it. I recently admitted to her on the phone that I've had a change of heart. I've shared with her that I've been doing a lot of soul searching on what my purpose is, and how I want to live my life versus how I've been living it. I told her I've cut back on drinking—a lot—and I'm feeling really good these days. She was of course supportive and said she's happy I'm happy. But I want her to *really* understand. Even more, I want her to go on this journey with me because I think she wants to... I think she's almost there.

We are so similar in a lot of ways—both success-oriented, both people-pleasers, both always up for a challenge. We ran our first half marathon together and she tackled a full marathon before I did, not to mention a couple of triathlons. She is also still single... still searching for Mr. Right. Or maybe her search, like mine, is really for something else. I have a feeling she also has a deep-rooted understanding that there's more to life than how we've been living. But I fear her second head is just as loud, if not louder, than mine. She is an absolutely beautiful person, inside and out, but for some reason she doesn't always see that in herself. That's something I think a lot of women struggle with.

I'm more afraid of talking to Taylor about it. Similar to my mother, Taylor will immediately defend *Me Then* to *Me Now*. She'll view this as me insulting the person I have been. She'll have my back, as she always has, and won't stand for me saying anything negative about the choices I've made or the life I've lived so far. She's a great friend and it will be difficult for her to let go of *Me Then*.

And I won't blame her at all. I'm fully prepared to be beer-bullied (because I've been quite the beer-bully myself). I wasn't just always the one who was down to have a drink; I was the one encouraging those around me to drink as well.

Let's have a drink.

Come on, just one more.

Why is it that when we're drinking, we insist the person we're with also be drinking? We don't do that with anything else. We don't pressure someone else to have a cup of coffee. When you really think about it, not only does it not make sense, it's outright strange. It's just a beverage.

For the record, I don't think there's anything wrong with drinking. Trust me, I'm in too much of a glass house to throw that stone. But I do question why I do it. Why is it my normal, but not everyone's normal? As I start to realize the extent to which I've let other people's opinions or expectations impact my life, I can't help but question my relationship with alcohol. Is it another thing I went along with out of fear that I would be rejected if I didn't? Or is it my liquid version of dicksand? Just another way of losing myself; a different escape from confronting my true feelings; a way to drown my third head into silence.

Sigh. This is about the point where I would say, "I need a drink."

JOURNAL ENTRY: future date

MARCH 2017

This morning I got up to watch the sunrise again. I wasn't really expecting to. I went to bed later than usual last night and had decided it might be best for me to sleep in. But then I woke up naturally at 6 a.m. I thought about getting up and making coffee and starting my day, but I decided I needed to take the opportunity to sleep more. But sure enough, I woke up naturally again at about 6:40 a.m. I laid in bed for a while thinking and then a funny thing happened. I was mid-thought about what I was going to say in the morning safety meeting at work tomorrow, and out of nowhere I just got up. I didn't even consciously think, "Okay get out of bed now." I just did it. I laughed to myself a little afterwards, thinking it was a bit strange. Some part of me I wasn't aware of was clearly ready to get out of bed!

It was a beautiful sunrise and as I stood there with my coffee, watching the colors of the sky change—which changed the colors reflected in the shallow pools not far from my feet—I was so happy I'd gotten up to be there for it. I decided to go for a long walk afterwards—it was a beautiful morning and the gym isn't open on Sundays, so at least I would get some steps in. I debated what to listen to on my walk and ultimately chose light classical music so I could give my mind the quiet it needed to think, rather than listening to someone else sing or talk.

As I walked down the beach, thoroughly enjoying my decision to walk, as well as my choice of music, my phone dinged its alert for a text message. I figured it was my mother, as she's the only one who would text me so early on a Sunday.

I was wrong...

Shane

Good morning!! Hope you're having a great weekend

I was surprised and yet not surprised at all. I doubted I would even hear from him after Easter, thinking maybe the small rejection of me telling him not to reach out until then would be too much to handle. But I wasn't *that* surprised, because it is common human behavior—especially when it comes to male humans—that as soon as you can't have something, you want it even more. I thought about not responding, but that just isn't the person I want to be. I hate being ignored, and even though he arguably deserves it because that's what he's done to me... several times... I didn't want to be that person. I didn't want to make him feel how I felt. But I also knew I had to stay strong.

I opened the calendar app on my phone and brought the view up to show the entire month instead of the week. I took a screenshot and sent it to him, saying: *Please note it is not April 17.*

I felt good about that response. Direct with a side of snark.

Shane

Oooooops my bad, just saying good morning

Thanks for the date update

I turned up the snark a bit:

No problem. For future reference your phone has a nifty calendar app that will tell you the date anytime you need to know.

Shane

So I can't say good night and sleep tight until April 17th?

That's been his go-to way of saying goodnight to me ever since I've known him—"sleep tight." Those two words bring back so many memories of being in bed and texting with him during all our in-between times, not knowing what was going on, or where it was going, but just feeling excited that we were talking. What is it about this man that has always had such a hold on me?

I decided to lower the snark and increase the directness: *Correct. You don't get to unilaterally decide when we are and aren't communicating. If you get to decide to abruptly stop, I get to decide if/when we start again.*

There—let's see if he goes down that road and remotely addresses what happened.

Shane

Okay, well good morning anyways!!

Yeah I said it

And I hope you're having a great morning

Nope. Not taking the bait. Part of me was disappointed

and frustrated. I just wanted him to apologize for what he'd done, acknowledge how unfair and disrespectful it was, and icing on the cake would be to offer some kind—any kind—of explanation. Another part of me felt happy he didn't. I don't want that conversation happening over text. I need to see his eyes to know if what he's saying is guarded and flirty, or vulnerable and sincere.

And the last part of me smiled and laughed a little. I immediately thought back to a road trip with Taylor about 6-7 years ago. We drove from Ft. Lauderdale over to Tampa to see her nieces and go to an FSU football game. On the drive back, she was texting with her then boyfriend, who's now her husband. There was something she was upset about and called him out on—I can't remember what it was, but I remember thinking that her feelings were warranted. He replied back with a dick pic. She laughed but I was angry on her behalf. *How dare he not take her seriously! She's upset and that should matter.* That wasn't Taylor's thought process though.

I asked her, "Doesn't that make you mad?"

She replied, "No, I like that he doesn't take everything so seriously."

At the time, I couldn't have disagreed more. I would have picked a fight over that. But that conversation and that memory has stayed with me. It used to pop back up every now and then when I was dating Shane because he was the same way. Sometimes I would get mad because I thought he wasn't listening to me or giving credit to my feelings, etc. And other times, I would think Taylor was right. Is this really something to get upset about? As you get older and go through and grow from different relationships, you learn to pick your battles. You learn to not nitpick everything. You learn to stay more focused on the bigger picture. But there's a thin line between doing that and letting someone walk all over you.

And Shane was walking that line.

I responded:

You must still be drunk from last night. Either that or you just refuse to respect my wishes. Honestly I hope it's the former.

Shane

It's neither, I was just saying good morning!! It's not like I'm asking you to coffee.

Now, I know Shane. That coffee comment is his way of testing the waters. In the past, I may have agreed to meet him for coffee under the condition that we talk about what happened between us. He would have agreed and then he'd be getting what he wanted—to see me. Not today. I followed his lead and didn't even look at the bait. Instead, I responded: *No more texts for a month. Please.*

Shane

Okay

>2 minutes<

Shane

I was going to ask to hear your voice but I'm sure that's a no

Unbelievable, right? He can't handle it. He can't handle not getting what he wants. Especially from me, who for two and a half years has always responded, and always been available to hang out. All he had to do was ask and I jumped. (Trying not to feel pathetic and sick to my stomach as I type that.)

I went fishing again:

Sucks to want to hear from someone you care about and they deny you that, huh?

Shane

Of course

I was just asking

Ugh.

My phone starts ringing—Facetime call from Shane.

With butterflies in my stomach and a pain in my heart, I denied the call and texted:

You've got to be kidding me

My phone starts ringing—a regular call from Shane.

As his smiling face stared at me, I really wished I had removed his picture from his contact entry in my phone. And as I type this, I remember that I did! But when my number was ported over to a new company phone, several settings reverted back to who knows how many months ago. Double ugh. And go-figures.

I silenced the call and rode out the 30 seconds or so of just looking at his face, memories flooding my brain.

I got more forceful:

I'm not answering. I don't understand why you can't just do what I ask.

Shane

I hit the wrong button the first time

I just wanted to say hello

I knew what would get him to stop:

You're about to make me mad.

He can't stand upsetting me, mad or sad.

Shane

Okay never mind

I don't like when you're mad. I apologize.

See?

I reiterated:

I don't like being mad. So please just stop texting me and don't call me. I won't answer. Just please respect what I'm asking.

Shane

I will, I was just wanting to say good morning

Now, even though he said he wasn't still drunk from the night before, this conversation was leading me to believe that wasn't exactly true. It's hard for me to believe that sober Shane would press this much and just keep saying the same thing over and over again. Both FSU and the Gators had March Madness games last night. One of Shane's good friends, who is a big drinker, is an FSU fan—and the chances are high that they went somewhere to watch the games. And quite possibly over-indulged while watching.

Recognizing this, I knew I had to spell things out, so I texted:

Okay. But you won't again until April—correct?

Shane

That's correct. Are you allowing me to say good morning now?

Oooommmmmgggg. At first, I thought he meant *from now on* and I felt like I was talking to a child. As I re-read it, I think he meant now as in *today*, wanting to know that his good morning today was accepted. Oops. Still, I responded strongly: *OMG no! (finger emoji pointing up) You WON'T again until April. Do not text me, call me, or FaceTime me again for a month. I don't know how to be clearer.*

Shane

Hahahaha. the finger thing is funny

Okay Kacie

He was either drunk or just determined to keep the mood light.

Either way I needed to go, so I texted:

Thank you. Goodbye.

Shane

You're welcome. Hello & goodbye

Exhausting. The man is emotionally exhausting.

As I continued to walk down the beach, having turned around mid-Shane conversation so I was now heading back home, I started imagining our conversation in April, assuming he reaches out. This wasn't the first time I've imagined this conversation.

In this daydream, I get right to the point because otherwise he'll try to chit-chat for too long. If he immediately asks why this had to wait until April, I'm ready to respond, "That's very personal, so depending on how this conversation goes, maybe I'll tell you." Then I'll get right into it:

I want you to know I get it. Recently I've taken time to really reflect on my life and figure out why I'm here and redefine what I want out of life. I now know what it's like to be super-focused on achieving something. To feel determined and want to spend every waking minute working towards something. That's how you operate—that's how you were with your business and that's how you were with remodeling your condo. I never really got it before but now I do. But in no way does that justify or excuse you for—once again—just disappearing and ignoring me. You ghosted me like we were 22-year-olds who met on Tinder. The last conversation we had was sexual via FaceTime. Then all I tried to do was see you before I went out of town—I wasn't applying a lot of pressure—and you just didn't respond! I was legit worried about you and told you that, and you didn't respond! It was F-ing Christmas and nothing! And then you text me months later asking about a sleep app?? Please tell me you have some attempt at an explanation.

Then I would listen. And I would ask questions. And if/when given the chance, I had a couple of other prepared statements:

The biggest mistake you ever made with me was bringing your guard down. Because now I know what that looks like. I know who you are and I know when you're not being that person. You don't even have to speak—I can see it in your eyes.

I will always love you. Those weren't just words when I told you that. But I don't know how I could ever trust you again. I can forgive. But how am I supposed to ever trust that you won't do that again? Hurt me again?

And, finally...

I can't be your friend. I will always wish you the best and, if we run into each other, I will smile. But this conversation can't be part of our usual pattern where then we start texting, then we start hanging out, and then you freak out and disappear. I don't want to hear from you after this.

I can see the conversation. I can hear myself saying the words. The question is—will this conversation ever take place? Or better yet, will I say what I want to say? I feel like I can. I feel like I'm finally in a place where I don't *need* him. Where I'm happy just as I am.

JOURNAL ENTRY: a burst of energy

MARCH 2017

I listened to a YouTube video yesterday—*How the Mind Influences Reality* on the Your Youniverse channel—and it connected a lot of things for me. I didn't even intently listen to the entire thing; I just had it on while I was making dinner. Then this morning while I was working out, I started thinking about a couple of things said in the video and my mind was a little blown when I connected all of these dots...

Everything living grows. One could argue that growing is all anything exists for—plants grow to provide food for animals, clean the air, etc. Animals grow to become food for other animals and some pollinate plants, etc. All of nature grows and interacts in perfect harmony. It all makes sense.

And then there's humans. We have to grow to produce

other humans—growth sustains life.

Growth is energy (well really, everything is energy, but stay with me). The act of growing is energy. According to Quantum Physics, energy exists in two forms—particle (physical) and non-particle (not physical, i.e. sound waves, light waves, and even thoughts).

Not all living things grow equally. Most living things (plants and animals) are limited in growth, both particle and non-particle. As far as particle/ physical—a tree will only grow so tall; some things grow in cycles (or seasons) where they grow and then die and then grow again. But either way, there is a limit to their physical growth. As far as non-particle— they don't have much growth; they don't seek out learning new things—they operate on instinct. A lion will never decide to be anything other than a lion. A pelican will never decide it wants to stop flying and walk everywhere. They aren't conscious of their thoughts like we are. That's what makes humans different... the whole "I think therefore I am" thing.

Humans, similarly, are limited in our physical growth (I'm not counting getting fat). But different from plants and animals, our non-particle growth is not limited. This is where self-improvement and personal development and everything I'm experiencing come in. We stop growing physically, but we can always continue to grow our minds. We can always learn different things, overcome barriers, create new habits, etc.—non-particle growth.

And back to my earlier point that everything is here to grow. That's what we are here to do also. To keep growing.

And if you accept that, then you can conclude that when you're not growing, you're not truly living. Certainly explains why I wasn't in a good place— my body is done growing but my mind craves more. Intuition, gut—whatever you want to call that feeling that something just wasn't right—was my desire to grow. It was my mind outgrowing my current life.

I can't explain how freeing it is to figure that out!

So many self-improvement and personal development teachings say that what you put out into the universe affects what comes back. "If you think it, it will happen" type stuff. Now I've shared that I used to really mock this concept but that lately I've somewhat changed my mind about it. I changed my mind because I noticed a change in my own life and my own world. But the concept still felt a little "fluffy" for me, and now I know why I couldn't quite accept it. It puts too much emphasis on the universe—like it's a separate thing reacting to us.

But if everything is energy (E=MC2), then everything is connected... and it always has been. It makes total sense. Nothing ever really goes away; it just changes its form of energy. A tomato seed grows into a tomato plant; you then eat that tomato; it is digested and some of it is taken in and absorbed by your cells. Now part of that tomato is part of you; the other part moves through your digestive system and comes back out in another form (okay I'll say it—poo). Maybe you're on a camping trip so you have to pop-a-poo—it's then absorbed back into the soil and that soil fertilizes a flower; that flower produces nectar, which attracts bees... and so on and so on.

My point is that there must be a finite amount of energy in the universe because none of it ever goes away. It just changes form and cycles around. It is all connected.

So just like growth in the physical (or particle) form interacts with and changes the environment, could you not make the same argument for growth in your mind (or non-particle form)? If thoughts are energy, then that energy is connected to everything else and therefore also interacts with and changes its environment. So if you change your thoughts, you can change your environment. We create the change. The change is us. It is not the universe reacting to us. It's all the same thing.

Mind seriously blown.

So, then my mind goes to another question: *Where did the energy come from? What started it?* Perhaps that's where God (or Something More) comes in. And if God (or Something More) *is* in fact energy, and therefore created all energy, and all energy is here to grow, and growth interacts with and changes the environment, then that explains everything from answered prayers and the Fibonacci spiral to *The Secret* and the "if you think it, it will happen" stuff.

Maybe the Bible actually was a way to explain Quantum Physics (a.k.a. energy, a.k.a. God) in a simple, analogy-based way like the child prodigy said.

My issue over the years with self-help and personal development "stuff" has been not understanding the *how* and *why*. I'm realizing more and more that I need to understand the how and why of things in order to fully engage with them. So with affirmations or things like writing what you are grateful for each morning, and all those other tricks or strategies you hear about... I never bought in because it's never explained in terms of the how or why. How or why am I supposed to believe that writing down three things I'm grateful for each morning will make an actual difference in my life? Why would writing down my goals and reading them each day have any effect on me actually achieving them?

But now I understand—it's because those actions and those intentional thoughts focus more energy towards what you want. Repeatedly thinking about and picturing what you want is all energy that has the ability to affect your environment. If you've always thought one way, changing that MUST have an impact. That energy has to go somewhere. It's now science. Not just blind faith.

That's another issue I have with organized religion—it asks for blind faith. Like we shouldn't question things past a certain extent; we should just accept them. But I think that isn't giving humankind enough credit. We SHOULD know the how and why. Questioning things is important. Learning is growing. It's how you leave the herd. We aren't meant to be sheep. Or at least I know I'm not.

JOURNAL ENTRY: the wrong side

APRIL 2017

Tomorrow I'm flying up to D.C. to visit my sister
Courtney, her husband, and my baby nephew. I'm
beyond excited to see them all. But driving home
tonight, I had a thought—she's going to ask me about
what happened between me and Shane in December.
I haven't yet told her or my mother. As far as they
know, we were seeing each other again and then all
of a sudden, we weren't... and I haven't wanted to
talk about it. I've been looking forward to telling
my sister about all of the realizations I've had lately
about trying to live my purpose and be more in touch
with my true self... I hadn't thought about having to
answer the Shane question. But I know it's coming.

I don't want to retell that story. And to make it worse,
I don't know if that's because I don't want to think
about it and relive it, or if it's because I don't want

her to think badly of him. I hate to admit it, but I think it's the latter.

Why do I feel the desire to protect this man who has twice abandoned me? Is it because on some level, I think there might be a round three? It's definitely possible that my brain would work like that. But I like to think it's because... with no agenda of us getting back together... I will always care about him and think he is a great man (despite his abandonment tendencies). I think I fear that people don't really know him like I know him and too easily judge him by things that absolutely do not define him. And that upsets me and I feel the urge to protect him.

Why can't I just say all that to my sister?

My mind is pulling up a memory of a tough conversation we had in our childhood bathroom at our parents' house. I was living in South Florida at the time and she was living in Charlotte. I can't remember why we were both visiting; perhaps it was Christmas time. We were both putting our makeup on and had somehow started talking about my relationship with Charlie. We were no longer together, which explains why I was willing to talk about the relationship. Within minutes, the conversation turned heated.

She argued that I was wrong to shut everyone out, especially her. I quickly and forcefully argued back that I didn't talk to her about it because she of all people—my sister—was supposed to support me and not judge me, no matter what. Yes she could disagree with my decisions and voice that, but she wasn't supposed to take a stand against them. And that's exactly what she did.

I admitted that I was absolutely wrong to have been with a married man. There was no denying that. But that wasn't my point. My point with her was always that she should have been on my side, trying to help me navigate the situation from a nonjudgmental, understanding perspective. I didn't need another mother during that time. I needed a sister. A sister I could talk to without getting a lecture in return. A sister who at least tried to put herself in my shoes instead of one who kept telling me to take them off. A sister who didn't look at me with pure disappointment in her eyes... I had enough of that.

We were both frustrated, and then it slowly clicked for her and she began to see my side.

"You're right," she said... her brain moving faster than the tone of her voice could keep up—the "you're" still filled with frustration and the "right" slightly softened into agreement.

And then, standing right where we used to spend hours playing Barbies… where we got ready for school together for ten years… she promised to always be on my side moving forward.

But I'm not sure I really ever let her back over.

JOURNAL ENTRY: baby on board?

APRIL 2017

I made it to Courtney's house in D.C. When I got here last night, I was a little taken aback—she was on the couch with her laptop doing work while Mike was up putting Nathan to sleep. That's not what surprised me—my brother-in-law is an incredible dad and out of all the couples I know, they do the best job of evenly splitting all child/household responsibilities. What surprised me was the lack of pure joy and excitement over seeing me. My sister loves me to death. She gets so excited when I come to visit and has a running campaign for me to move wherever she's currently living. But last night, she was like a shell of herself. Excited, but too exhausted to feel it. And when my brother-in-law came downstairs from putting the baby down, he was the exact same way. I had never seen them like this. Parenthood was weighing on them.

My entire life, I've said I wanted children. I love kids. Kids like me. I'm good with kids. I wanted to be a child psychologist. One of my goals written in the back of *The Last Lecture* is "have a baby."

I remember once questioning this... I even said it out loud to a couple of people. My reason for questioning it at the time was the state of the world—so much violence, so much destruction (both physical and moral). Don't even get me started on technology... social media with the selfies and bullying, the pressure young girls feel to look a certain way, and the clothes and products that are being marketed to them at such a young age... it's all disheartening. I remember one day thinking about the direction this world seemed to be heading in, and what I would likely experience in my lifetime, and then I thought *why would I want to bring a child into this?* It seemed like a selfish act. I voiced that to a friend or two and they didn't really have a strong reaction either way. I voiced it to my mother and she was horrified. "Don't be ridiculous," I think she said. I decided maybe that was an over-dramatic way of thinking so I went back to the "I want kids" mentality.

The problem with that mentality is that it starts to apply a lot of pressure on getting married. I've never been the girl that planned that part of my life—

"I want to be married by 28, have my first baby at 30, yada yada yada."

"I want to get married on the beach and my wedding dress will be all lace."

"My bridesmaids will all wear periwinkle blue and the groomsmen will have matching bowties."

Nope, not me. I've never had a single detail of a wedding or husband planned out. I've only had blanket statement plans for my life like, "I want to get married and I want to have kids."

Well, I'm now 32. I'll be 33 in less than two months. Ever since I turned 31, I've caught myself sometimes doing very dangerous math in my head...

I would like at least two kids because I love my siblings, so assuming I want to have the second baby by 38 at the latest, due to the increase in health risks after that, that puts me having the first baby by age 36, and I would like to be married for at least two years before that so we have some "us" time, so 34... and I want to date someone for a couple of years before we get married... Shit—I have a year and two months to meet someone, fall in love, get engaged, and have a wedding.

Pretty sobering math equation.

And to throw an extra wrench into the situation, it turns out that getting pregnant isn't as easy as I was always afraid it was when I was sleeping with guys I would never want to procreate with. I've known so many couples who get so excited to start trying... and then it doesn't happen... and doesn't happen... and doesn't happen. What an emotional rollercoaster. Each month your hopes get so high, and then you're disappointed time and time again. I'm sure the magic of it all starts to fade as your sex life gets put on a strict calendar, you go for test after test to see what's wrong with you, and ultimately you end up conceiving your child in a petri dish.

My brother and sister-in-law were one of those couples. After they did IVF, they were told it didn't take—they weren't pregnant. We later learned Kimberly actually *was* pregnant, but the doctor's office had somehow misread her results so that both her and my brother were unnecessarily devastated for a full 24 hours before the mistake was realized. I went over to see them the day they got the bad news to try to help console them. I walked in and first hugged my brother; his face carried a sadness I've never seen in him before. I went out to the porch where Kimberly was sitting, eyes puffy from hours of tears. We started talking and she made a comment that it wasn't fair that she wasn't pregnant. And it's so easy to see why she would feel that way—they had been through a lot trying to get pregnant. But for some reason, that comment triggered something inside me... something I rarely feel—anger. There were so many things I was thinking but dared not say.

Not fair?? You've lived a charmed life for as long as you can remember. A life where you've probably gotten everything you've wanted from childhood to adulthood, where you are now able to choose not to work because it's too stressful. I'm so sorry you can't just say you want to get pregnant and POOF you're pregnant right when you want to be. Look around you. People don't get what they want when they want it. And I'm so sorry you've been praying every night and you're frustrated that God hasn't just responded immediately to fill your request but last time I checked it doesn't work like that.

Luckily, I didn't let any of that show. I sat there calmly, nodding my head and listening, and responded with something like:

"I know it's really tough. But I'm going to tell you what I told Courtney when they were going through this—never lose sight of what you do have. You have a husband who loves you and a marriage that has actually gotten stronger from going through this hard time. This kind of stuff breaks a lot of couples and instead it has brought you closer. Not everyone has that and that's an incredible blessing."

Me saying this carries an emotional weight she can't ignore. Because I'm older... and single. Me saying this helps put things slightly more into perspective for her—that just because life isn't going exactly according to her desired timeline, that doesn't mean it's a bad life.

(For the record, I love Kimberly and she has the most genuine and wonderful heart. My silent rant was not a reflection of how I feel about her, but instead a projection of frustration with my own life onto her situation. Who am I to assume she's gotten everything she wanted out of life? Of all people, I now understand that someone's life on the outside doesn't always reflect the truth of what they've been through or who they are.)

There was one interchange in that conversation though that really stuck with me. Kimberly was talking about how much she wanted a baby and, with big tears in her eyes, she said, "I mean, all every woman ever wants is to be a mom. It's why we're here."

And deep down inside me a voice—maybe my gut!—responded *not every woman*.

I quickly attributed that thought to my inner feminist who doesn't believe that every woman does, or should, want to have children. I'm not sure there's a worse situation than people having kids when they don't actually want them.

But when I talked to my parents the other weekend, one comment my mother had was that my life can't be *all* about others—"What about getting married and having kids? Is that no longer in your plan or part of your purpose?" she asked.

My initial reaction, which I didn't say out loud, was *no*. And that caught me off guard too. I thought about it for a second and found a way to articulate it to my mother… "It's not that it's not part of my plan. Yes, I would like to get married and have kids. I hope it happens. But I can't control that…"

(I paused as I started to tear up so I could compose myself.)

"I'm just taking the pressure off of myself."

"And you should," my dad chimed in.

These surprising gut reactions, coupled with seeing my sister struggling last night, have me thinking about whether or not I could make all of the sacrifices involved with having children. I was wrong to think it would at all be selfish—it's the most selfless thing I've ever seen.

A couple of my college friends have had babies but they all live in different cities so I never directly saw the impact it had on their daily lives. I only saw all the cute photos shared on social media. My South Florida friends don't have kids yet and my Jacksonville friends for the most part are all younger than me with no kids. My sister is the first new mom I've really seen firsthand. Before she went into labor, I was so scared for her that I thought I was going to cry. But she did it—like a champ. I was in awe of her. And immediately obsessed with baby Nathan— he was this little bundle of perfection. But the most incredible thing was watching my sister transform into a mother in an instant. Just like that. She had this calm confidence about her while handling this tiny baby that just amazed me. It was hard for me to wrap my brain around it at first—she was never the baby person when we were growing up; that was me. I wasn't even sure she liked kids! But there she was—this adorable, natural mother.

And now six months later, juggling work, baby, husband, house, and her sanity... she had lost that new mom glow. Hell, she had lost any kind of glow. It broke my heart to see her like that.

I couldn't help but wonder… though I dared not ask anyone but myself… is it worth it? Could I give up all my routines that I love? All the time I have worked so hard to dedicate to myself? Could I give that up for someone else? And better yet—do I want to? I feel like I'm finally back on track with my life, but there's a damn biological clock ticking that will one day force me to decide if I want to do what seems like derailing in order to accommodate having a baby.

For the first time in my life, I'm *really* questioning if I want kids.

JOURNAL ENTRY: meeting in the middle

APRIL 2017

Today while Courtney and I were getting pedicures, exactly what I was afraid of happening happened...

"So what happened with Shane?" she asked timidly, like someone trying to get close to a skittish animal, fearing they'll scare it away.

Her face was so full of hope that I would open up to her. How could I disappoint that sweet, hopeful face looking at me? I just couldn't. I took a deep breath, and then I just let it all out...

The Christmas disappearing act.

My "this is the last time you'll hear from me text" and then my "are you alive?" text. (eyeroll)

Writing "should I?" in my prayer box when I thought

about reaching out to him months later for closure, and then hearing from him several days later after the run.

Being strong and telling him to contact me after Easter.

Hearing from him (again) and reminding him (again) not to contact me until after Easter.

My prepared statements for if/when we do talk again.

I even confessed that I was afraid she was going to ask me about him, and how I don't understand why I feel the need to protect him.

She quietly listened, never interrupting. Probably still scared the skittish animal might take off.

Her lack of interjecting with argumentative questions, eyerolls, or looks that said "Are you kidding me?" allowed me to keep talking... probably to the point of rambling... reiterating several times that nothing excuses how he treated me, but that I still think he is a good guy. Outsiders can and have looked at the situation and said there's another woman or that he's just an asshole, but I *know* that's not true. He's just scared.

Overall I surprised myself with my candor (the wine

might have helped). And she surprised me with her response. She didn't question or lecture me in any way. Instead, she looked at me and said, "I'm happy he surfaced during a time in your life when you are feeling more in touch with yourself."

She went on to say she was proud of me for how I was handling it so far, and that she trusted me to make the right decisions for me moving forward… and that whatever they were, she would be on board with them.

It was a true sister response. I doubt she agrees with my "he's just scared" justification. And I doubt she wants him back in my life. Whether or not my doubts are warranted doesn't matter. What matters is that she is on my side.

JOURNAL ENTRY: walled in

APRIL 2017

Today I had so many great moments with my nephew laying on the floor with him on his play mat, just watching him smile and stare at me, grabbing at my face trying to get to know it better. My heart melted. I had a thought that I've had before but I always brushed away as nonsense—*I'm scared of how much I would love my own children if I had them.* I can't imagine handling that amount of love. I see it in the way my mom looks at me—it's almost like a pain. Looking at Nathan looking at me... and loving him so much... I can't imagine what it would be like if he was built from me; if I had given him life, grown him inside me, and literally brought him into this world. And then I thought *how can I love this tiny person so freely and let him love me back, but I'm unable to do that with the adults in my life?*

As the day turned into night, my sister got visibly more upset, knowing my departure tomorrow was getting closer and closer. When I said goodnight, she said, "I love you." I replied that I loved her too, but mine sounded nowhere near as heartfelt as hers. And I *do* love her. So much! Why can't I even just say the words without sounding guarded? All she wants is for me to bring my walls down... and not just in terms of talking about certain people and events in my life; she wants me to bring down my overall emotional walls... and I just can't do it.

The night I first got into town, when I told them my story about the YouTube video and my determination to reconnect with my true self, she came over and kissed me on the forehead. Why couldn't I reach out and embrace her? Why did I instead feel awkward and uncomfortable, and then guilty that I felt that way? (sigh)

Earlier today, she made a comment about it being a great visit with love and sadness in her voice, and I just agreed and moved the conversation along. Why couldn't I delve into the memories and how much they meant to me? I don't know why I emotionally hold back with the people who love me the most. As soon as they get vulnerable with me, I close up. I feel it happen and I try to stop it, but I can't. I'm sure on some level it hurts them, and I hate that.

The walls exist physically as well. I used to be so much more affectionate. I remember as a child and even up into high school, I would lay on the couch with my mother while watching TV and snuggle. I don't really let people touch me now, and I feel uncomfortable when they do. Even my close friends— it's so normal to hug each other hello and goodbye but I feel awkward every time.

When I'm in a relationship, touch is like a barometer for me—whether or not I *want* to touch them, and whether or not I want them to touch me. Even little physical displays of affection feel fake and forced to me if the emotional connection isn't there. I remember always wanting Shane to touch me. When we first started dating, he would all the time; not obnoxiously, but just in very subtle ways just for me. Like sitting at dinner and placing a hand on my knee. Or walking by me and gently touching my waist. Or by reaching out in the middle of the night to pull me a little closer. I can't shake those moments. When the realities of life came between us, all of that went away. I've seen glimpses of it over the years on nights he's been drinking, but for two years I've just wanted him to hold me. *Really* embrace me. That's the unguarded truth.

Why does that desire for closeness exist for him, but not the people in my life who actually choose to stay in my life? The people who consistently show me and tell me they love me?

I can't help but think maybe my emotional walls are actually the cause of the pain in my life, not the result of it. Maybe feeling off track all comes down to not being in touch with myself... my gut... my emotions. If I haven't been connected with my true self (my third head), how could I possibly connect with others? All this time, I've been focused on what other people think, how they feel or don't feel, what they are doing, and how that's affected me... when really, I should have been looking at me, figuring out what I think, how I feel or don't feel, and what I'm doing, independent of everyone else.

My walls don't just keep others from getting in, they're keeping me from getting out.

JOURNAL ENTRY: a daily struggle

APRIL 2017

Discipline is no easy task. For the most part, I live a pretty disciplined life—I work out consistently, I meal prep on Sundays so I have healthy lunches during the week, I remove my makeup and do my face routine every night (no matter how tired or drunk I am), and I don't let dishes pile up in the sink. But higher-level discipline—being disciplined about doing what you know will make you happy in the long run, not in the moment—that shit is difficult.

My discipline had a test this past weekend with my sister. And while I by no means failed miserably, I wouldn't exactly say I succeeded either. I ended up drinking way more than I meant to on Saturday... not to mention I completely forgot about my "no liquor" Lenten promise and ordered a margarita at lunch (oops). I did do a little bit of writing, so that's good.

I didn't work out... well, I didn't even bring workout clothes so I really set myself up for failure there.

I was thinking on the plane ride home about why it's so hard to do the things we know will make us happier in the long run. Why do we always choose short-run happiness instead? I want to choose to live the life I truly want in every decision, even the small ones. I can feel the result of not doing that this past weekend. Right now I feel less happy, less inspired. It's so easy to make little allowances here and there, but I know how those little allowances can add up and before I know it, I'll be off track again. I can't have that. And I need the people in my life to know I'm serious. To know this isn't a phase; this is me being me.

This morning, when my sister and I were both getting ready—me to fly home and her to go to work—she told me she thinks my writing is a really healthy outlet for me, but to try not to let it stress me out. She said I shouldn't put a lot of pressure on myself to do it. I responded, "Well, writing a book is a goal of mine and reaching your goals often requires some stress—like training for the marathon was stressful." She agreed but somewhat reluctantly, like I wasn't seeing her point. But I know her point—that a hobby shouldn't be stressful. And we didn't get into this but had we, my counterpoint would be that this is more than a hobby. This is me actually pursuing something I've always wanted to do. Like, for real. And it's a big goal. And it's scary because it won't be easy, but I'm all in.

I know it will be a process for people to understand the changes I'm pursuing in my life, and I will constantly have to reframe things to try to help them understand my perspective. That is what I have historically failed to do. I let my perspective get lost. I would give up on it the moment it got frustrating to explain it to someone else. I don't want to go back there.

I still worry about the reactions of some of the people in my life. I even had a dream last night that Taylor pretty much stopped being my friend because I didn't want to party as much. I don't foresee that being her reaction at all. I know she loves me. But I also know she will question me on this... not from a negative place, but from a protective place. She'll see it as me straying away from who I am (instead of the opposite). And I can't blame her for that. She's only known me to be someone who was always down to go out, always one of the last ones standing at the bar, always down for fun. When I strayed away from that in the past, she blamed external forces. She has no idea there was an internal voice involved... and that's no one's fault but mine.

Most of the people in my life know me as a party girl.
One of my cousins and his family were in D.C. for
their kids' Spring Break this past weekend, so they
came over to my sister's house on Sunday to see us
and meet Nathan. When talking about their plans
for the week, my cousin made a comment to me that
we had probably spent all weekend hanging out at
bars instead of "doing tourist stuff," while rolling his
eyes. His comment wasn't meant as an insult—more
an acknowledgement that I would consider tourist
stuff to be lame. But the comment stung a little. It
wouldn't have before—the first time I went to visit
Courtney and Mike in D.C., I specifically told them I
didn't want to do any tourist stuff; I only cared about
seeing the social scene. Oh man was I wrong. We
passed the White House while walking to dinner the
first night and I looked at it in awe of all the shit that
has gone down in that house over the years. We biked
the National Mall and I fell in love with the Lincoln
Memorial. Turns out, I love the "tourist stuff" in
D.C. But my cousin wouldn't assume that; based on
his knowledge of me, he was correct to think that I
would rather have been at a bar.

I no longer want to be known as someone who would
rather be in a bar than experience the art, culture,
and history of our nation's capital. And I certainly
don't want to be known as someone who would

choose to be drinking at a bar versus home snuggling with my baby nephew. That small comment made me realize the extent of the perception I've created of myself... and how difficult it will be to change it. But I think changing *my* perception of myself was harder. So at least I'm over the biggest hurdle.

One motivational speech said the key to happiness is to make progress every day. Progress makes us feel energized and happy. I didn't make progress this past weekend. I should have gotten up earlier to write or work out before Nathan woke up. I should have gotten up one day to watch the sunrise over the monuments I love so much. I didn't do those things. And on the plane ride home, I did not feel happy and energized. I felt a little disappointed in myself. I realize now that I will constantly be tested at really living my words. And my next big test is right around the corner...

My annual cruise with my MBA friends.

JOURNAL ENTRY: real talk

APRIL 2017

Have you ever asked your parents about their lives? Not about one specific time, but more about why they made the decisions they did. I did that today... maybe for the first time ever.

I spent the day at my parents' house—Kimberly, my mother, and I laid in the sun by the pool while my brother and dad golfed. When they were done, we all hung out for a bit before Alex and Kimberly left to go home. I stayed to have dinner with my parents. I knew my mom was worrying about me and feeling like I'm not spending any time with her, which equates to a fear that I'm shutting her out. We sat on the porch chatting and I remembered a question I had for my dad which I randomly thought of earlier this week.

"Why did you decide to leave your job as an engineer

to go to law school?" I asked, almost out of the blue.

I know the basic timeline of my dad's life—he went to FSU and graduated with an engineering degree; he got an engineering job and married his college sweetheart; he left the engineering job and went to law school; he got divorced from his college sweetheart; he got his LLM in taxation from NYU; he married my mom; his small local law firm merged with a very large national firm; he had three kids; etc.. But I didn't know the *why* behind most of those decisions.

He started to tell me the chronological story of his career, and every so often I would stop him and ask him "Why?" Too often, I think people only tell us, or maybe we are only interested in, the *who, what, where,* and *when.* But the *why* is the best part. The *why* is how people think and who they really are. As we were having this conversation, I couldn't believe that it took me this long to ask these questions and hear his story. But as I think about it more, it's not surprising—it's taken me this long to ask and answer all the *why*'s of my own life.

I'm like my dad in many ways. People always say I'm just like my mother because we're both high energy and have a lot of the same mannerisms. But my brain is a lot like my dad's. So when I wonder why he never proactively told us about his life/career in all the years we were growing up, I immediately know the answer—he's not one to tell you if you don't ask. I'm the same way. I'm much more comfortable talking about other people and listening to their stories. I must get that from him.

As he told me about the different chapters of his life, and I kept interjecting questions to understand his reasons and the thought process behind his decisions, I wondered how he felt about this conversation. Was he thinking, "I can't believe she just now at 32 wants to know about my life"? My hope is that he was happy I cared. Happy I cared to ask one question and even happier every time I wanted to understand more. I learned so much about this man I have known my entire life, this man that gave me life.

I was all ready to do the same exercise with my mother, but the conversation took off in another direction before I got a chance. And it went into really interesting places—we went from leadership styles and what really drives people, to presentation styles and politics. It was one of those rare, really great conversations where everyone is equally contributing, telling relevant stories, sharing and learning from each other. It was the kind of conversation that makes my brain happy.

Too often, I find myself in conversations about things that don't really matter. We talk more about what's happening in popular TV series than we do about what's happening in our own lives. And this feels especially true in today's toxic political environment. We avoid talking about anything political or controversial for fear that the other person has different views and it will turn into an argument. It's really upsetting. How can we ever learn and grow from each other if we aren't even really talking to each other?

I was so grateful for the *real* conversation tonight. After I left, sure enough, I got a text message from my mother:

Thanks so much for spending so much time with us tonight! We love you so much and love being with you. You are so very special!

Special. I like that word a lot more than different.

JOURNAL ENTRY: on purpose, *part 1*

APRIL 2017

This morning on my way to work, I was thinking about the great conversation about my dad's life and I regretted not asking him what he thinks his purpose is, which I've always assumed to be financial. Now I recognize I could be totally wrong. If I asked him, he might say something very different. My dad is actually a very emotional man, although few get to see that side of him.

While thinking about my dad, I also thought about Shane. I hate how he randomly pops up in my mind, but he does and always has, ever since I met him. Maybe it's because I heard from him recently; maybe it's because I never seem to get closure in all our back-and-forth; or maybe it's because, for some reason, I just can't get over him. (I don't know how I feel about that one—Mad? Sad? Confused? Pathetic?)

Shane is also seemingly driven by money. In the beginning of our relationship, when I was still living in South Florida, we had a phone conversation about the business he was starting. It's always stayed with me and I'm not sure why. He explained to me the number of jobs he would have to do for a certain profit—doing all this math out loud as I tried to follow him—and that if he could meet this goal, he would be at $100,000 for the year. I remember that conversation as clear as day. I even remember exactly where I was driving—Pine Island, in the lane to turn left on Broward Boulevard. Out of all the phone conversations we had, why do I remember that one so clearly? At the time, I was surprised by his very specific financial goal. Maybe that was because I wasn't setting specific goals for myself; maybe it was because that sounded like a ton of money to me; maybe I was just surprised that he was so financially focused. I saw the money fixation more and more as I got to know him and at first, I just thought he was determined to make his business a success. I later realized it was really all about dollars in the bank and I never understood why. I also never tried to understand why.

I got some clarity about a year ago when I randomly heard from Shane after one of his longest hiatuses from my life...

LOOKING BACK: paying attention

AUGUST 2016

AGE: 32

I had been in a relationship with Adam for about
six months. Adam is the guy I was out with when
David first confessed his feelings. He's the kind of
great guy who everyone likes. You could literally
place him in any social scenario and he could survive
and have fun without any hand-holding. He's smart
and attractive and I really wanted to be into that
relationship. But something was just missing for me.
We had a fun friendship, but that was all it was. I
tried to convince myself otherwise, telling myself I
wasn't giving him a fair chance and giving myself
pep talks that friendship is the best foundation for a
relationship. But deep down I knew I was forcing it.
And right around the time when that knowledge was

bubbling to the surface, I was at a work event with April and my phone dinged for a text. I nonchalantly looked at it, expecting it to be Adam or my mother... nope. It was Shane.

"Holy shit," I said out loud, staring at my phone with a face I can only imagine held a combination of shock, panic, and delight. I hadn't heard from him since I'd been with Adam... literally, the last time I heard from him was the first night Adam and I hung out together. He drunkenly wanted me to come over to his place. I surprisingly said "no" to him (yay go me!) because I was out and having fun... and called him out for only wanting to hang out with me when he'd been drinking. He responded by asking me to go to dinner with him the following night. I agreed. Then I never heard from him the next day... or for the next six months.

And in true Shane fashion, he just once again texted me out of nowhere like nothing had happened, sending me a picture of the DVD of the most recent season of *The Walking Dead*, "our show" that we used to always watch together.

(Ironically, it was Charlie who introduced me to *The Walking Dead*; I then introduced it to Shane and he loved it; and then I used to watch it with Adam as well, feeling almost guilty, like I was cheating on Shane. Eyeroll. Apparently on some level, I equate being in a relationship to the zombie apocalypse.)

"What??" April asked, looking at me just staring at my phone, not sure if I'd just gotten amusing or worrisome news. I wasn't sure either—should I be amused that Shane had just resurfaced right when I started to really question my current relationship, or be worried that this would only lead to more heartache?

April knew some of my history with Shane at that point, but not the entire story. I quickly gave her the CliffsNotes version and we talked about what, if anything, I should respond. She knew I was conflicted in my relationship with Adam, and after hearing me explain the Shane story, she was perceptive enough to see I wasn't over him. And she didn't judge me for that—another reason I love my friendship with April. She doesn't try to impose her (or society's) definitions of what a relationship or love should look like upon anyone. She just seeks to understand. I'm sure that's because she's encountered her fair share of people who've chosen to judge her rather than try to understand her. Maybe that lack of acceptance is what taught her how to truly be accepting.

I responded to Shane, playing along with *The Walking*

Dead bit for a couple of texts, and then I cut right to the chase—calling him out on nonchalantly texting me, acting like nothing had happened. Like he hadn't asked me to dinner and then just disappeared... for six months.

I was surprised by his response. I had prepared myself for him to either skirt around the issue or just go silent and ghost again. But he did neither. He recognized that a lot had happened, and said he wanted to get together to talk about it. Quite different than the text conversation the other day when I was walking on the beach.

We made plans to meet up that night to talk about everything. I wasn't sure if he knew I was seeing someone and I felt like I was doing something wrong by meeting up with him... and I didn't tell Adam. He had his fantasy football draft that night so he was busy anyway. And luckily he didn't ask me anything about my night, so I wasn't put in a position to either lie or tell the truth. But I still wonder if not telling him was some form of a lie or not fair to him.

On my drive to meet Shane, I was shaking with nerves. My heart was pounding. I felt very conflicted...

What if he says he wants to be with me? What do I say?

Stay strong. You're with someone.

But I love him.

But he will just hurt you again.

Maybe it will be different this time.

You said that last time. And the time before.

But...

Right when I got out of the car, he told me I looked nice. A seemingly small compliment to most, but to me, it was so much more. For as long as I've known him, he's always had a way of complimenting me when I need it most—when I've felt insecure in some way. It's like he has some kind of radar for it. And it's always felt so sincere. I loved how it made me feel. And considering compliments made appearances about as often as a blue moon in my current relationship, it was exactly what I needed.

I told Shane almost immediately that I was seeing someone (he hadn't known) and he seemed surprised. I also picked up on just a hint of sadness. As we talked about our complicated past, he told me something about himself I never knew before—well he had made comments, but I never knew the extent of it. He talked about how he had gotten into a lot of financial trouble in his 20s. He foreclosed on a condo, was living paycheck to paycheck, and at times couldn't afford to pay his bills or go grocery shopping. He vowed to himself that he would never be in that position again. And after witnessing his work ethic while getting his business up and running, I doubt he ever will be. He poured everything he could into it—every waking hour. He explained the stress and pressure he felt to never go back to that point in his life; the obsession with his account balance, and how if it ever got below a certain point, he immediately thought he was going to lose everything again.

So on the surface, you could easily say his focus was on making money. But as I think back on this conversation, I realize that's shortchanging it... it was much deeper than that.

Shane has mentioned to me before that he wants to have something to leave his children. His dad is a hardworking man and did the best he could, but they didn't have a lot of money growing up. And then a bad divorce with Shane 's mom dealt a big blow. So needless to say, there is no nest egg for Shane's dad to leave to his sons. Shane and I have the same financial advisor—Peter, the brother-in-law of one of my good friends from college. Peter once told me that Shane said he "wanted to change his family tree."

Changing your family tree—now that's a great purpose.

Again it comes back to the "whys" of our lives being the most interesting part of the story, but we rarely focus on those elements. I knew Shane was super-focused on work when we were together, but I never really asked why. All I did was look at how it affected me; how it prevented me from getting what I wanted. But his "whys" are wonderful—he was super-focused on work, yes. Why? Because he wanted it to be successful. Why? Because he never wanted to be broke again. Why? Because he wanted money to leave his children. Why? Because he wanted to change his family tree.

I wish I would have asked those "whys" when we were together. I wish I would have dug below the surface of his busy schedule and had more real talks with him.

JOURNAL ENTRY: on purpose, *part 2*

APRIL 2017

As I think about it, I get a little frustrated with myself that I'm just now putting this all together. I bet my dad's purpose is similar. My dad's dad was a painter in Chicago until they moved to Florida and opened a motel. They didn't have nice things or take nice vacations. I'm pretty sure my dad was the first in his family to go to college. And when he left for college, I always imagined he sped away without glancing in the rearview mirror once. My dad's relationship with his parents always made me sad, as they didn't seem very close. But maybe my dad's purpose was also to change his family tree. Maybe he sped away and didn't look back because he was so focused on looking forward. It would explain why he at times was so opinionated about my college or career choices. It was because my success was wrapped up in his purpose... in his "why" for everything he has accomplished in his life.

He really needed me to succeed and just wanted me to go about it in what he knew to be the best way. It also explains why he gets so emotional when talking about his children as adults now—all of us graduated college and have good jobs. We are proof that he fulfilled his purpose.

Or maybe he wanted to have a closer relationship with his children than he had with his parents. And to him, closeness meant providing direction. I've been battling anger towards my dad for the direction he's provided me in my life and yet I never asked why he was providing that direction. Just like with my mother, all I saw was him trying to tell me what to do. But maybe it's much deeper than that.

I guess you can't ever really judge the way someone else lives their life, or even the decisions they make. Because you don't know where they have been or where they are going and why. You don't know the deeper reason, the purpose—the "why"—that's driving it all. Just like Hadley's dad said, we shouldn't beat each other up. Instead, we should seek to understand.

And maybe they don't even know the answer to their "why's" yet. Maybe they're just trying to figure it all out. Like I am.

JOURNAL ENTRY: continental divide

APRIL 2017

I did it. I just registered for a volunteer trip to Africa. I'm going to Tanzania for two weeks in September. As of now, I'm going alone, but there's a chance my mother might come with me. I brought it up to her the other day when we were laying out by the pool. She said it's something she would like to do but felt concerned about the timing since my dad's 70th birthday is in September and in October she's going out of town with her college friends. She doesn't like to leave my dad several times in a short timeframe—she feels guilty because she thinks he won't have anything to do. She may be right. It's funny how men get so dependent on their wives. Especially extremely smart and successful men like my dad, who in their younger years "played the field" and were seen as the type that might not ever settle down. It's like once they do, they really do.

She asked if there were any other dates to go on the trip and I explained that there were, but we couldn't go in November because that's Kimberly's due date, and then December is Christmas, and I don't want to wait until next year. There's no guarantee that we'll be able to go in January—what if Kimberly has a very complicated birth? What if the baby comes early and she needs extra help for the first couple of months? Who knows what else could happen between now and January?

Earlier today, I texted her that my contact at Global Volunteers (the organization I decided to go with) informed me there are only two spots left for the Tanzania trip in September.

Mother

Okay. Courtney was thinking we should host Kimberly's baby shower Labor Day weekend because a long weekend makes it easier. Would that be an issue?

I looked up when Labor Day is this year and, of course, it's the weekend we would leave. Ugh.

I responded:

Yes—Labor Day is September 4th and we would leave that Saturday, September 2nd.

Mother

Maybe it's a sign we should wait until January.

I took a deep breath, feeling that infrequent emotion—anger—start to move in. Not because what she said is unreasonable, but because of the bigger context that comment lives in. And I made that very clear:

No. A long weekend only makes it easier for people coming out of town… that's probably only Courtney. I always do things according to everyone else's schedule because everyone else has things going on like weddings and babies. Well now I have something going on—it's not a baby or a wedding but it's important to me. Courtney didn't come to Christmas one year so she could go to Africa with her friends.

I really don't think I'm overexaggerating—over the years, I have rarely missed a family event, birthday, holiday, vacation, wedding, wedding-related activity, etc. Granted, I recognize it's easier for my schedule to accommodate all these things because it's just that—*my* schedule. I don't have to coordinate with anyone else (a.k.a. a man). But still. It's only fair that every once in a while my life gets to influence the calendar.

And I remember how upset I was about my sister missing Christmas to go to Africa—(1) because I'm a big holiday tradition person and already had to adjust to only getting my sister at every other Christmas, and it was the year after Alex got married so I was adjusting to the idea of some Christmases not having either of my siblings there; and (2) because in my mind, Africa was *my* trip. I've always said I wanted to go; I had never heard her once say she did. It was my goal, not hers. But she happened to make friends with someone from South Africa and all of a sudden she had to take my dream trip *and* miss a family Christmas on top of it. I realize that's some obvious sibling rivalry. And of course that exists on some level with me and my siblings. But with my sister, it's more complicated because I've followed her life... and I don't think that's because I wanted to. It's because I didn't have the strength or willpower to go out on my own. I wanted to go out of state for college but ended up going to FSU, where my sister was, and rooming with the little sister of my sister's best friend, and joining the same sorority as my sister.

And it doesn't stop there—after graduating, I moved to South Florida, where my sister lived. Now in my defense, Taylor was from there and moving back, and I had made other friends who lived there so it *was* where I wanted to go... at least, I think it was.

My sister and I have had a rocky relationship at times over the years, but the past couple years have been great. I know I don't share as much with her as she wants me to, but I'm working on it and she's more understanding with me about it. And it's not that I'm trying to make my sister's life more difficult, but when you put things into perspective, there are a lot of weekends we could throw Kimberly a baby shower. And I want to go on a trip of a lifetime that's been a desire of mine for as long as I can remember. I'm pretty sure my schedule gets precedence in this case.

My mom's response to my text was simple:

We can pick another date for the shower.

I know I got what I wanted but I felt a pang of guilt reading that. I don't want to be difficult... a voice in me is saying *you really could push the trip back, it's Kimberly's first baby.* But it's that thinking that has gotten me where I am today. And I know that. Which is why I won't let it happen this time.

A little later, I sent my mother another text:

I'm going to register tonight. I have to do this for myself for many reasons, it's very important to me and I don't want to wait. I can't keep waiting to do the things I want to do because I don't have someone to do them with. I'm comfortable going alone and I completely understand if the timing doesn't work for you. I won't be upset. I have a feeling this won't be the only one of these I go on.

She didn't respond. I don't think she is upset; I think she just wants to talk to my dad before responding. We'll see I guess.

Either way, I'm going. Deposit paid. Goals "Go to Africa" and "make a difference in an underdeveloped country'" will be completed this year. Boom.

JOURNAL ENTRY: a masters in fun

APRIL 2017

This morning I was thinking about the upcoming cruise with my classmates from my MBA program. I love these people. They made one weekend a month in Gainesville (a.k.a. enemy territory for this FSU girl) something I actually looked forward to. I will admit I wasn't the best student in my MBA program. I took a similar approach to the one I had in undergrad—put in the least amount of effort possible to get better-than-average to good grades. I wonder if I would have been a better student in a Psychology graduate program. Oh well.

Regardless, I excelled in the social element of it. I would drive down Friday afternoons, usually leaving early from work. I loved the drive there—I would listen to the New Music Friday playlist on Spotify, which was how I would find new songs I liked for

my running playlist or my more mellow driving
playlist. Friday nights I would spend alone in my
hotel room. I love hotel rooms. Always have. I would
almost immediately get in my pajamas, get in bed,
and find a movie on TV. Sometimes I would have
last-minute work or studying to do, but most nights
I just enjoyed a night alone away from home with no
pressure from anyone to do anything, and nothing
to do except be lazy. Saturday was class all day. We
were all creatures of habit so everyone usually sat in
either the same exact seat or at least the same general
vicinity. I always had a really entertaining circle
of friends around me to suffer through class with.
I laughed a lot and I loved it. On Saturday nights,
there was a core group of us who would always go out
to the bars. On Sunday mornings, class started even
earlier and we always looked rough and felt rough.
But we laughed about stories from the night before
and people who didn't make it to class; and people
would disappear for an inordinate amount of time in
the middle of class to either nap in their car or on a
sofa in one of the building's lounge areas.

We had a great time. After we graduated, we went
on a cruise to celebrate. We had so much fun that
we decided to make it an annual event and we're
following through with that commitment—coming
up is our second annual cruise. My identity in this

group is definitely a party girl. I was the only girl in the backrow cracking inappropriate jokes and talking sports. I was one of only a couple of girls in the group who always went out on Saturday nights. I was "one of the guys" and I loved being one of the guys. I guess I can still be "one of the guys" in my newfound desire to live a different life, but I can't be the party girl. I can't be the girl always down to get another drink, take a shot, and stay out longer.

I'm really struggling with how to let go of that within this group. There's a very loud voice in my head saying *just take a weekend off—what's the big deal?* And another voice that answers *because then you're being weak, reverting back to your old ways that you know make you unhappy... plus, you know you'll feel like crap afterwards and regret it.*

Which voice do I listen to?

Ideally I can drink casually throughout the cruise—not so much that I feel like crap, but not so little that it's obvious. I'd love it if I got up at a decent hour each morning and either enjoyed some time on the deck, perhaps saw a sunrise, read, or worked out. I want to bring my computer and continue to journal like I've been so disciplined at doing too. But I'm rooming with my friend Brooke and I don't really want to explain why I felt the need to bring my computer and write during a party cruise weekend with people I only see once a year. I will be very honest on why I'm hesitant... I'm scared about what they'll think of me. I'm scared to lose my "status." I'm scared they won't think I'm as much fun. I'm scared they will like me less. There, I said it. What no strong-willed, confident person likes to admit—I'm scared to do what I want to do because of what other people will think.

My second head sure isn't going down without a fight.

JOURNAL ENTRY: mind change

APRIL 2017

They say it takes 30 days to change your subconscious mind. Well, thirty-four days ago the "what's your purpose" video punched me in the gut, starting me down this journey. And tomorrow begins my biggest test—the cruise with my MBA friends. Can I be the person I want to be or will I fall back into old habits and old thought processes?

I think I can do it. I can be the real me on this cruise and not succumb to peer pressure or the desire to be liked and seen as the party girl. The thought even crossed my mind to give up drinking altogether. One thing this growth spurt has given me is a whole new appreciation for my mind—from what it's currently capable of to what I know it is actually capable of. And one thing I know for sure is that my hungover mind is not capable of much for a solid day, and then gets very sad. I don't want to feel like that anymore.

Driving to work this morning, I was flipping through the radio stations and I got a little annoyed. One station was having people call in to say what they were mad about. Another was talking about the latest celebrity gossip—some drama about one of the Jenners and a Pepsi commercial. I got so irritated. This is what we are talking about? Calling radio stations to say why we are mad? Holy negative. And some drama-tastic family that is famous for no reason? This is the information we are sharing? I haven't been on social media for over a month but I can only imagine what's going on in that realm. How did we get to this point where that's what people are interested in hearing? Radio stations aren't dumb—they're fighting each other like crazy for listeners so they can get big advertising dollars. And I'm sure they're spending big money to figure out what will get those listeners. And this is what their market research has come up with? And it's not just radio—look at TV shows. How many shows do we have that are literally just focused on us watching other people live their lives, usually in some ridiculous or abnormal circumstances? Now, I love movies and I get the whole mindless activity escape thing but... come on.

I feel like so much of what we talk about or are

interested in is on the surface. No one asks me what my dreams or aspirations are for my life. Yet on the regular I get asked what shows I'm watching. Or if I saw a recent sporting event or awards ceremony. And to be fair, I haven't been asking people these deeper questions either. We constantly ask, "How are you?" and we answer, but how often is it a *real* answer? It's usually "I'm good" or "I've been busy" and then we move on. We never ask questions to dig to the next layer—the how and the why—and then the layer below that. We seem to do that better when talking about other people's lives more than our own. Whether gossiping about celebrities or people we know, we will analyze the shit out of their lives, actions, motives, and emotions.

Are these all distractions from talking about what's really going on with us? Keeping the focus on other people so we don't have to deal with our own deep-rooted feelings that are oftentimes scary or uncomfortable or sad?

On social media, we're sharing results from quizzes that tell us what actor we should be dating or what state we should be living in... or posting where we are drinking, or what we are eating, or trying to sell each other the latest multi-level marketing scheme. Social media is supposedly all about connecting us, but are we really connecting? The only times I see posts on any subjects deeper than how much someone loves their best friend on their birthday are usually something political about why someone else is completely wrong. That's certainly not connecting.

I feel like we aren't *really* talking to each other—we aren't sharing what's really going on with us. I know I certainly haven't been. Everything stays surface level where it's easy and comfortable. The deepest conversations I've had over the past couple of years were usually preceded by a lot of alcohol. And if we aren't really talking, if we aren't really being *real* with each other, how can we possibly really connect with one another?

I can't live on the surface anymore. I can't do it. I want conversations that matter. I want real talk. I want to actually connect with people.

I'm sitting here thinking about what I want out of life… I think I want even more. A lot more. Today the thought crossed my mind that maybe I can change the world. I'm not sure how yet, but it's a feeling I have deep inside.

Oh, and my mother is going to Africa with me. (smile)

JOURNAL ENTRY: 1st, 2nd and 3rd head—all aboard!

APRIL 2017

I am on the cruise ship as I type this. My roommate, Brooke, is asleep in the adjacent bed. I'm proud of myself for booting up my computer and typing this despite how tired I am... and admittedly, a little drunk. So to be completely transparent, I'm just going to type some notes now and then come back and fill this entry in. I'm having a little trouble typing and I may or may not be closing one eye in order to read what I'm writing.

Today was a bit of a roller coaster. I drove down to the cruise port with the rest of the group that lives in Jacksonville—Brooke, Tony, and his wife, Lauren. On the drive down, I told them everything I've given up for Lent—figuring I might as well get it out there in this small group first and see how it went. No shots for Kacie. I didn't go into a lot of detail, but I told them how I'd been doing some soul searching and hadn't really been drinking much.

Now remember—to this group, that news is likely shocking. But I was pleasantly surprised when Tony and Lauren immediately spoke up that they hadn't been drinking much either, so they understood and were totally on board (pun intended) with my Lenten promises. I let out a big sigh of relief in my head.

The conversation then got a little deep. We started talking about work and how to figure out what it is you really want to do. Brooke has been job searching recently and Lauren said she really hasn't been enjoying her teaching job. (So many people are unhappy in their jobs.) I told them about the mental exercise I was given by the hiring manager for the job I didn't take. It was a really good conversation. We talked about career paths and how easy it is to end up in a job you never set out to have, and how then it just gets harder and harder to take a risk and pursue what you really want to do. Pretty sure that was the most real conversation I have ever had with Tony and we spent one weekend a month with each other for more than a year.

It was awesome to see everyone when we got on the ship. Most of them I hadn't seen in an entire year but it felt like it was just yesterday we were on the same ship celebrating graduation. A couple of life update conversations and, before we knew it, it was back to our old times of telling stories and laughing.

A few hours into hanging by the pool deck, most people had switched over to liquor drinks or frozen cocktails. It wasn't long before I was called out by my friend Jack, saying he was surprised I was still drinking beer. They all know I'm a vodka girl, or should I say vodka purist—vodka and water with a lemon and a lime.

I confessed that I gave up hard liquor for Lent. "So you're going to drink beer the whole time?" he asked, both confused and surprised.

"Well and wine," I said shrugging.

Not long after that, we all went to the Windjammer for a snack before heading back to the rooms to get ready for the night. At this point, a couple of very strong margaritas had several members of our crew feeling really good. As I sat there with my beer still in front of me, Aanya (the wife of one of my classmates) asked why I was drinking beer.

(Side note—isn't it funny how we not only give each other a hard time about drinking, but about *what* we are drinking as well? It's like we all have to be doing the same thing at the same time. It's weird.)

Someone was quick to chime in that I gave up liquor for Lent. Aanya's face turned to pure disappointment. She was on the cruise with us last year but she was pregnant. She told me how she had been telling her husband how much last year sucked because she couldn't drink with us and how she—and I quote— "just wanted to party with Kacie." She looked legit sad. I laughed it off and explained that she shouldn't worry, I would still be drinking—just not liquor. "Lent Kacie sucks," she sighed as her drunken eyes found her drink and she took another sip of her margarita.

And there it was. Exactly what I was afraid of. I tried to brush it off. I told myself she didn't mean it. But inside, a voice was telling me to *just cave.*

An hour or so later, we dispersed to our rooms to get ready. Brooke immediately passed out on the bed. I woke her after I got out of the shower so she could start getting ready. She got up and threw up. She was one of the margarita victims. She lay back down, looking like she felt like shit, and said she needed to sleep more. I stood there looking at her, knowing exactly how she felt, and feeling so grateful that that wasn't me. In fact, I felt reenergized about sticking to my plan to pace myself and prove that I could have just as much fun maintaining a nice buzz instead of going down my vodka party path.

There were a couple of jabs about my liquor hiatus throughout the night, but they were all in good fun and, for the most part, nobody cared that I had wine at dinner instead of a cocktail. And then I had a great conversation with Ronin.

Ronin and I became very good friends during our MBA program and we have stayed friends ever since. I've gone to visit him and his wife, Luna, who is also on the cruise. Ronin likes to challenge people on their decisions—not in a negative, judgmental way, but in a desire to understand and sometimes poke holes in the logic behind those decisions. He asked me how I was doing in a way that I knew was really asking me to explain why I've given up so many things for Lent. I gave him more detail on what's been going on in my life—explaining that I've been defining my purpose and really looking at how I live my life and trying to determine what really makes me happy versus what's just habitual thinking. He listened intently and nodded along.

When I finished my CliffsNotes version of the past month, he told me he was relieved, as him and Luna had been worried about me. "We actually had a couple of conversations about how you seemed off," he said with genuine concern in his voice. "It wasn't to the extreme that you sounded suicidal, but like it had the potential to go down that route."

Suicidal. I cringed at the word. The three of us have an ongoing group text and I had told them I wasn't in a good place a couple of times, but I never imagined they would be legit worried about me to that extent.

"No, no," I quickly replied. "It was nothing like that." But as I said it, I felt a little bit like I was lying. Don't freak out—I never actually thought about harming myself in any way. But in my apathetic state, certain thoughts did cross my mind that I knew weren't normal...

I don't really care about being here.

Would it matter if I wasn't?

My family would be devastated.

I could never do that to them.

And that's as far as it ever got. I've never told anyone those thoughts.

We then started talking about drinking and he pointed out that, if I really pay attention, I'll see he never gets drunk. I looked at him somewhat confused, thinking back through all the nights when we were out late in Gainesville.

He said he sips on drinks and orders shots for everyone but makes a point to never get drunk. He views it as being at some kind of disadvantage.

Interesting I thought to myself. I never noticed. I always just assumed he was on the same level as me and everyone else.

Our conversation was then interrupted by the group because it was time to hit the casino. "We'll get back to this," he said to me as we got up from the dinner table.

I hope so I thought, happy to have an ally on the boat.

JOURNAL ENTRY: a deeper dive

APRIL 2017

Aanya (the "Lent Kacie sucks" girl) has three friends on the cruise, all of them guys. They're fun and fit in nicely with the group. They all know each other from working at the same gym—Aanya and one of them are personal trainers. I found out this morning that they all went to the gym before breakfast. They were out with us last night and they still got up and worked out. So it can be done! I asked one of them if I could join them tomorrow morning and he said I could. (Yes, I brought workout clothes on a cruise. A first.)

After breakfast, we spent the day in Nassau. It was a great day! We chartered a boat from a local (as opposed to through the cruise ship) and toured Nassau; then we stopped to snorkel; then we went to this little beach with not many people on it. We had coolers of beer and snacks and I was able to easily nurse my beers without anyone noticing or giving me a hard time.

While getting ready for dinner though, I started to feel very confused. How do I distinguish between what I want to do, what I'm programmed to do, and what I'm meant to do? And does the feeling of *want* really come from within my true self, or does it speak up for what I want others to think of me? I'm struggling with how to live the life I want for me versus the life I want to have perceived by others. How do I know which is which?

I've always been a person of extremes—all or nothing. So again, I ask the question—where is the balance? Is the balance drinking moderately on this cruise? Or is the balance the fact that I only see these friends one weekend a year so why not get drunk with them like I used to? Is that sound logic or is that making a small concession for my 1st and 2nd heads? I honestly don't know.

Basically, I'm having a hard time letting go of the party girl persona. And not worrying about other people judging me for it.

I felt frustrated with all of it as I sat down to dinner. When the drink waiter got to me, I ordered vodka. I didn't really think twice about it. Oops. My justification to myself was that I woke up that morning with a headache from drinking wine the night before, and I knew my vodka water drink would not do that to me.

The night was fun—most of the guys gambled in the casino while the girls bounced around the ship, popping into the club to shake our booties for a bit. There was one conversation during the night I found interesting—a couple of us were sitting in the bar outside the casino chatting. Something came up and I made the comment that I've gotten really interested in energy. Luna and Jack were immediately intrigued and asked me to elaborate. The three of us started to have a fun conversation about how if everything is energy, then everything is connected, and what all that means. I was loving it. And then Brooke interrupted with the famous "Let's take a picture." Oh, how I haven't missed saying that.

I want to have these real conversations with my friends. I want to discuss things that matter—who they really are, what they want out of life, what they question, what they find interesting, and why... the "how's' and why's" of their lives. What I'm finding out is that some people are willing to go that deep and others just prefer to stay on the surface and take picture after picture.

I'm not going to give up. These are my good friends.
I want to really know them. It's time to dive in.

JOURNAL ENTRY: woman overboard

APRIL 2017

Oh boy…. where to begin.

A lot happened today so I'm going to run through it quickly…

I did get up and work out with the guys. The one who is a personal trainer was too hungover to get up so one of the other guys, Ryan, trained me and their other friend. I'm pretty sure he underestimated my workout abilities because it by no means kicked my ass, but it felt good to get up and break a little sweat. And of course, thanks to my vodka, I didn't feel too hungover.

After the workout, we met up with the rest of the group at breakfast. They all laughed and joked about how I went to the gym and was now going to eat a protein bar—it was all in good fun and didn't bother me at all. So far so good.

And then as we were hanging out on the deck before we got to Coco Cay, I had a great conversation with Aanya. It started with somewhat normal girl talk—"You look great; what have you been doing?" I explained that I just hadn't felt like running after the marathon and had been focusing more on weight training. As a personal trainer, she was all for that switch. She then dove right into her struggles as a new mom and finding time for herself. On top of taking care of her baby, she was caring for her ill mother. She got emotional talking about her stress level and how it was wearing on her. I was actually a little bit surprised with how personal the conversation got in such a short period of time. We don't know each other very well at all, but she clearly needed to vent to someone and that someone was me. I guess Lent Kacie doesn't suck at listening!

I felt bad for her. It's such a common thing—not having time to take care of ourselves because we are busy taking care of everyone else. I see it mostly in women I know. We are so selfless. I can't help but think of an airplane. When the oxygen masks come down, you're instructed to put yours on first. Even before you put one on your child. Why don't we apply that same concept to life? We have to take care of ourselves first. It sounds selfish, but it's not. You can't give your best to *anyone* in your life if you aren't actually at your best. You're denying the ones you love the full extent of everything you have to give if you aren't taking care of yourself. Easier said than done, I know. But still something to think about.

Later in the day, Ronin and I continued our conversation from the first night. We talked about our purposes in life and our career goals, and he called me out on drinking vodka last night. He explained how keeping his word is extremely important to him. If he says he's going to do something, he will do everything he can to do it. I told him my justification, but he wasn't accepting it—"If you said you aren't drinking liquor during Lent, then there should be no reason why you would break that."

Damnit, I thought. *He's right.*

It was then I realized it's not so much about the drinking or what is or isn't balance—it's about keeping my promises to myself. Doing what I say I'm going to do. That's how you get off track—by not staying true to your word, to yourself.

Despite him blowing my vodka justification out of

the water, it was a great conversation with a great friend. No surface level there!

Now is where it gets juicy...

Throughout the day, I started to notice Ryan noticing me. After years of devoting a lot of time and focus towards men, I've developed a keen sense for when someone is just being friendly towards me versus other intentions. And on top of that, Jack and Tony told me they made a bet on which of the guys I would hook up with. I laughed them off, saying they were both going to lose. I was surprised by that bet—all the school weekends we spent together, I never hooked up with anyone. I guess bets like that just come with the territory of being the only single girl in a group. Story of my life.

The three guys Aanya knows were all Marines. Apparently, Ryan was injured really badly—"blown up" is the phrase I overheard in a conversation earlier in the weekend. The guys were all cute and fun, but I was having fun and really didn't want to deal with any boy-meets-girl crap.

When we first got on the boat, one of the initial things Aanya said to me was that her friends are really nice and she was especially excited for me to meet one of them. I immediately told her that I wasn't interested—that wasn't my intention for this cruise and plus I gave up men for Lent. I hoped that would be the end of it, but sadly I was wrong. Because now there was a big elephant in the room that I had to ignore. A puddle of dicksand I had to step around.

It became more obvious while walking back from playing beach volleyball when Ryan asked me the "So why is someone like you single" question. I hate that question. And I told him that. I gave him some quick answer about how I stay in bad relationships too long or something like that. I really didn't want to get into that conversation… or even think about it for that matter. This is my vacation. A vacation within a bigger vacation from all the men in my life. I certainly don't want or need to add any more players to the roster.

After Coco Cay, some of us went to hang out by the pool before it was time to get ready for dinner while others went to nap. Slowly but surely, the pool group started to leave to get ready and before I knew it, only Ryan and I were left.

What happened next I did not see coming. We were watching one of the crazy cruise poolside competitions, casually chatting, and then he took it to a whole other level. He told me he wanted to know all about me. That he's dated a little since he got out of the Marines, but he hasn't felt this drawn to someone in a long time, if ever. He told me he was impressed with my drive while we were working out, and how he's never met a girl who's so grounded. He said he can tell I'm closed off, but he really wants to get to know me. That's why his roommates were all napping and he was out by the pool—because he was hoping I would be here.

Oh boy.

I was completely taken aback. And even though I was only drinking beer, I was pretty buzzed at this point. I could tell he was interested but I was by no means expecting to be punched in the face with this level of honesty. Not to mention—huh?? We'd maybe spoken 47 words to each other prior to this conversation!

I didn't know how to respond. I was a little dumbfounded. I tried to sidestep his outright vulnerability and asked him how old he is, knowing he's younger. Wait for it... 24!!! He's only 24! That's just shy of a ten-year spread between us. When I was his age, he couldn't even drive yet.

I then proceeded to struggle through the conversation,

him pushing me out of my comfort zone with very personal questions while I tried to hide how uneasy I felt. I explained to him that I've been through a lot, and that I'm not in a place to even think about men/dating. I could tell he wanted some kind of response from me though—some answer to his unspoken question. Am I also interested?

So many thoughts were going through my head.

End this conversation immediately.

But he's cute and you're on vacation—YOLO.

He's 24!

So? Age is just a number.

I gave up men for Lent.

Lent is over in like two seconds.

Keep your promise to yourself.

More importantly, stop being so guarded.

I told him he caught me off guard and that I needed to process it all. He walked me to my room and we agreed to talk later.

I got into my room and just started laughing. *What the F just happened?* I didn't have time to think about it. I had to quickly get ready so I could meet everyone for drinks before dinner, as was our plan.

An hour or so later, we were all sitting around a big table in the bar playing Cards Against Humanity. Ryan of course snagged a seat right next to me. Now I started to pay more attention to him—how he moved with subtle confidence, how he quietly looked out for everyone—*Did they need another drink? Did everyone have enough cards? Did he need to jump up to get someone a chair? etc.*

Would I have noticed these things had he not expressed such blatant interest earlier by the pool? I don't know. But I definitely noticed them now. The elephant in the room had gotten bigger. And every now and then it whispered in my ear, pointing out how good it feels to be wanted, and how lonely I've been.

At dinner, he was across from me and next to Luna. Every now and then I discreetly listened in on their conversation—she asked him about the extent of his injuries from overseas and he explained that he'll likely be completely deaf by the time he's 35, but that he's okay with that. His acceptance and overall positive demeanor while saying that was impressive. I overheard something about me being mentioned but then their voices lowered and I could no longer hear what was said.

Later in the night, I was sitting with Luna at the club while the guys were in the casino, per usual. It was the first time during the weekend we had a real chance to talk just the two of us. She asked how I was doing and brought up how they had been worried about me. Maybe it was all the wine, or maybe it was a deeply rooted need to tell someone, to just say it... I don't know what it was about that moment, sitting in a dark club on a cruise ship and surrounded by strangers shaking their tail feathers... but in that moment, I shared with Luna what I had not yet said out loud. I explained how I never really thought about committing suicide... but I did think about how I didn't care that I was here. And how my best (and maybe only) reason to stay was to not upset my family.

There, I said it out loud. I never thought I would because I barely even acknowledged the thought yet I found the courage to say it out loud. And I'm so happy I did, and I'm even happier it was to her. Because her response was perfect. She didn't act surprised. She didn't look at me like there was something wrong with me. She didn't tell me to seek help. Instead, she connected. She just nodded along like what I was saying was totally normal. She shared that she too has struggled with depression. *Depression.* I never considered it that... but maybe it was. I feel like that's a taboo word in the world that I live in. Like depression only looks like withdrawn, quiet, exhausted women who can't leave their dark bedrooms. Not possibly energetic, smiling women who are running marathons and getting their MBAs.

Depression or not, it felt good to tell someone and get a reaction of understanding. Another example of how we should talk to each other more. Because no matter what we're going through, chances are good the other person will understand. Maybe even relate.

Not long after the seriousness of the conversation faded, she smiled and said, "So, what's going on with Ryan?"

"Ugh," I sighed. "I have no idea what's going on." I told her the whole story of what he said by the pool and how I was so shocked and now feeling really confused. Part of me was encouraging myself to just let go and have a fun experience and explore this situation, while the other part of me was rolling my eyes and saying *here we go again with the dicksand.*

We talked through it a little bit but her stance can easily be summed up—someone like Ryan who's been through what he's been through comes with a lot of baggage. Be careful. I might not want to deal with that, especially at this point in my life when I'm already confronting all my own issues.

I understood and explained to her that I'm worried I'm too closed off. I'm worried I don't give people a chance because I'm still not over Shane. I'm worried I'm too quick to find reasons to write people off. I don't want to be like that anymore.

The night continued on and was a blast—we played (and won!) the cruise scavenger hunt game. When all the bars closed, we roamed around the ship, ultimately ending up on the back deck where the basketball court and ping pong tables were. It was a small group of us at this point and slowly people started to peel off and go to bed. I had promised Ryan we could continue our conversation, so once again we were the last men standing. We sat out on the pool deck—by this time, it must have been around 3 a.m.—and continued talking. I told him I was confused and that this didn't make sense—"You're A LOT younger than me and we don't even live in the same city," I said, still feeling dumbstruck that this conversation was even happening. "What is it you hope to get out of this conversation?"

He said he simply wanted to get to know me. Even after the cruise. He had a genuine counterargument for all my concerns—*Orlando is a short drive from Jacksonville, age doesn't matter, there's no harm in getting to know each other.* He was so calm and gentle. So open with his interest in me—a feeling I craved from Shane for so long.

He walked me to my room and, in the tiny hallway of the cruise ship, another Lifetime movie moment ensued. Only this time, it was a totally cheesy one instead of a drama-tastic one. I could tell he wanted to kiss me but he was hesitating.

"What are you thinking?" I asked. Totally cliché girl move right there.

"I'm thinking about kissing you," he responded shyly.

"Then do it," I said.

And he did. And it felt great.

JOURNAL ENTRY: beware of dicksand

APRIL 2017

Well, I'm back on dry land. I woke up after only a couple hours of sleep and quickly threw all of my clothes into my suitcase, still flustered from last night, and we headed back to Jacksonville. I did not see Ryan this morning—their group got up and disembarked earlier than we did. We have been texting though. And he's already asking when he can see me again.

There are definitely some similar patterns here. A long-distance romance starting with a whirlwind weekend—sounds an awful lot like how Shane and I started. Both men are also complicated—with Shane, I didn't realize the extent of it right away but considering what Ryan has seen and experienced overseas, I know he is. One difference is that me and Ryan's conversations were much deeper, whereas Shane and I had really fun, witty banter. I wonder if

Ryan banters…? I do want to laugh. There are also similarities with David—the dedication to physical fitness, incredible discipline, deep analytical thinking.

Is this another test to see if I can break my unhealthy patterns?

The big difference is hopefully me. I'm certainly a different person than when I met Shane several years ago. I'm even different than I was thirty-something days ago when the incident with David happened. I can't help but feel this is a test. Problem is, I can't pinpoint what exactly the test is. Is it a test to stay true to my Lenten promises (which I technically already broke), where passing the test would be to cut things off with Ryan and tell him to reach back out after Easter? Seems a little silly since Easter is less than a week away at this point. Or is it a test to finally bring down my walls and explore this connection despite the societal judgements regarding age, and the logistical inconveniences of the long-distance thing?

I hope it's the latter. One reason for that hope is because Ryan very quickly figured me out and still pursued me. There's something to be said for that. That conversation by the pool shocked me so much because he saw all these things in me yet he barely knew me. The last decision I made based on someone seeing me for how I want to be seen—taking my current job—was a good decision. Perhaps the same decision-making process applies here. We met on a weekend when I was actively trying to be the person I want to be—that's the person he saw and he still wants to get to know me. That has to be a good thing, right?

My upcoming weekends are all booked except this very next one, which means we either see each other this coming weekend—which also happens to be Easter weekend—or not for like two months.

We've agreed on this weekend. Patience is a virtue I don't always have.

I still can't really believe this is happening, and I'm still feeling very confused. This weekend I *have* to be in touch with my gut. I need to quiet my mind and decipher how I feel when I'm with him. Quiet the pre-programmed thoughts about him being too young, and not wanting to get in a long-distance situation, and the added emotional baggage he brings from his days overseas. But also hold back the tendency to sink in the dicksand. I need to figure out if I'm actually interested in him, separate from his interest in me.

Confession—I would be lying if I said Shane wasn't

a small factor in deciding on this weekend for Ryan to come and visit. As much as I hate to admit it, I want to figure out what really exists between Ryan and I before Easter in case I hear from Shane. Not at all because I'm expecting things to start back up between us if I do hear from him. It's more that I know hearing from Shane will stir up a lot of confusion for me so I'd rather have some clarity with Ryan before that happens. I can only handle so many question marks at one time.

Why do I continue to let Shane play a role in my decisions?!?!?!

JOURNAL ENTRY: it's the end of my world as I know it

APRIL 2017

Last night I had a dream with a giant snake in it... and the end of the world was coming via a big storm. We all knew it and there was nothing we could do about it. The dream was very vivid.

It was an odd dream to have, one I've never had before, so I Googled the symbolism of dreaming about the end of the world. And wouldn't ya know... according to DreamBible.com...

To dream of the end of the world represents fundamental change to your ways of being and thinking. The foundation of your current life has been altered. It symbolizes your thoughts or feelings about a dramatic change or situation in life where you don't know what to do. You may be experiencing anxiety for the future, and there may be a lot of changes that confuse or frustrate you. The dream may indicate the end of one kind of lifestyle and the beginning of another. There may be a need for help or extra time to make adjustments. A sign you need to show more courage as you move into the next chapter of your life.

No F-ing kidding.

JOURNAL ENTRY: the tip of the iceberg

APRIL 2017

This morning while I was getting ready for work, the video I was listening to had a great explanation about how your mindset can bring about change in your life. It explained how energy harmonizes with like energies. So if everything is energy, then what you want out of life is energy also—everything from particle/material things like money to non-particle things like feelings (relationships). When you realize the things that you want are all energy, then you can work to harmonize your energy with the energy of what you want so that you attract it.

What does that mean exactly, or how do you do it? I'm not sure yet, but I still like it.

It said a key component of affecting change is to learn how to be grateful for what you want before you have it. You essentially trick your subconscious into thinking something exists that doesn't (yet), which in turn makes it strive to make it a reality.

Interesting.

I got to thinking... gratefulness is a feeling, not a thought. And this is not the first video to talk about the power of combining thoughts and feelings to change things in your life. There's something there; I just can't wrap my brain around it yet.

The video also had a great analogy to help explain the relationship between consciousness, subconsciousness, and the universe. Think of consciousness as an iceberg. What you see above the surface of the water is your conscious mind: what you are aware of. What is underneath the water—the majority of the iceberg—is your subconscious mind: what you are capable of but unaware of. The water that the iceberg sits in is the universe.

And what is an iceberg made out of? Water.

So just like an iceberg is a crystallization of water, we are a crystallization of energy and the universe. Because remember, everything is energy. And the energy of the universe—the water—has no limits. It's full of infinite possibilities. Therefore so are our lives. We just have to change our conscious mind, elevating more of it above the surface—crystalizing more of what we are capable of into reality or our consciousness.

It is our consciousness—our awareness of our thoughts and our ability to question them— that separates us from other living things. We can change our mind, which will change our path. A sheep will not question why he/she is in a herd. This unique ability of ours is what allows us to bring more of the iceberg out from underneath the water, getting it above the surface. Our ability to question things. And to find new ways of thinking.

But it is not easy. I recently heard an upsetting statistic that, on average, we have about 65,000 thoughts per day and 95% of those thoughts are the same as those we had the day before. This is because we are creatures of habit—we park in the same spots, drive the same route to work, etc. Our brain is built to pick up on patterns, and over the years we've created so many patterns for it that we are essentially on auto-play, living the same loop over and over again. We are on auto-play with small things like brushing our teeth and where we sit in meetings, right on to big-picture ways of thinking, like the pattern we have that after high school you go to college, then you get a job, then you get married, have kids, work more, and retire, etc. Our lives are planned out for us by the collective habitual thought patterns of the world we grow up in.

But what if we don't fit that pattern? What if we outgrow it? I think that's what's happening to me. All these habits (big and small) don't fit anymore. Auto-play certainly explains my apathy. How can you feel fully engaged in your life if you also feel like you don't have control, like you're just along for the ride?

But here's the good news—even the slightest change in those habits or patterns can open our minds up to new possibilities. That's been the past month or so for me. Changing some habits and questioning some patterns has opened my mind up to so many new possibilities that excite me. New possibilities that don't fit the collective thought patterns of the world I've grown up in.

This process of even contemplating who we really are, what we really want, and what we are capable of begins to open our minds and elevate our consciousness. And the more we raise our consciousness, the more we realize that the limits we have set on our lives and our abilities do not actually exist. We are capable of so much more. Not only do we have to realize that and know it... but we have to *feel* it—the power of thought plus emotion.

The video also made an interesting point about how, in a limitless mindset, we can't decide *how* something is going to happen. We often set historical limits on our lives based on how things have happened in the past. But we shouldn't focus on *how* something will happen. We should instead focus on what we want and why, and keep an open mind as to how it will arrive. That, of course, made me think of Ryan. In wanting a companion in life who I connect with on an intellectual, spiritual, and physical level, I would not expect that person to arrive in the package of someone who's eight years younger than me. And my historical limits would tell me that an alpha male with emotional baggage who lives in a different city will only end in heartache and drama. But I can't let the past dictate the future, and I can't close my mind to the avenues by which life will give me what I want.

Maybe Ryan is the result of me breaking my patterns and opening my mind.

Or maybe he is me on auto-play, blindly walking into dicksand. I guess time will tell.

JOURNAL ENTRY: MAN-ifesting

APRIL 2017

I was driving home from work today, feeling happy and excited for the weekend. I had a renewed sense of positivity about Ryan coming to visit tomorrow— looking forward to hopefully just having fun and figuring it all out. And then *BAM*—I drove right by Shane. Saw him clear as day.

What. Are. The. Chances??

There are layers of irony in this...

First of all, it's Easter weekend. Easter weekend last year is when I hung out with Adam for the first time *and* heard from Shane for the last time before his six-month disappearing act. He resurfaced right as I was starting to really doubt my relationship with Adam. And now I've met someone new and I'm trying to give it a fair shot—and I see him. I drive that route every single day on my way home from work and I've never driven by him before. Why does he come back into my life during times that hold some significance around another man?

This is a pattern that goes way back...

Go back to when I was probably 28-29 years old and I was dating Charlie. One night, my sister's friend texted me that she knew I had a boyfriend but that her boyfriend had this friend who she really thought I would get along with—that friend, of course, was Shane. To this day, I remember getting that text and being annoyed she would send that, knowing I was with someone. Later that same night was when I saw on Facebook that first love Lloyd and his wife were having a baby and I burst into tears.

Fast-forward maybe close to a year—I was at the tail end of my relationship with Charlie, but I just couldn't totally let it go. He had moved back in with his family, but for some ridiculous reason, I couldn't move on. I went home for Christmas and I went to a Jaguars football game with my family. That same friend of my sister was coming to join our tailgate. Unbeknownst to me, she was bringing Shane. My family all knew about this "set-up" and no one told me. They were all for it because they were all desperate to get me to move on from waiting for a married man to leave his family for me. Shane and I had a fun interaction but we both went our separate ways when it was game time and that was it. I'll admit I caught myself looking for him in the stadium bar at halftime hoping to see him, but I didn't.

Four months later, I was back home for—you guessed it—Easter weekend, and my sister's friend texted me a picture of her boyfriend and Shane, saying, "Look who I ran into! I know you're in town this weekend, so can you come meet us out?" I was tempted to go meet them but was deep in a drunken game of Cards Against Humanity with my family and couldn't muster the energy to change out of my pajamas.

A couple months after that, I was finally over the Charlie relationship and had joined eHarmony in an attempt to "get back out there." I had a good first date with one guy, with plans for a second date, and wouldn't ya know it—Shane got my number from my sister's friend and reached out to me. He ended up coming to South Florida to visit me that weekend. I had the second date with the eHarmony guy on Friday night and Shane arrived on Saturday. During that weekend, we hit it off. Big time. I immediately ended things with the eHarmony guy and the rest is history.

Man, there's clearly something about Easter weekend and other men in my life that brings Shane out. The coincidence in all of this is unreal.

I used to believe in "meant to be"—not necessarily that we all have "the one," but more that certain things are destined to happen. But with everything I've been thinking about and realizing these past forty-something days, "meant to be" doesn't hold any water. Everything that happens in my life is either a habit or a pattern I haven't yet broken, or else it's the result of an intentional change I've made. I'm in control.

So does Shane pop up in these seemingly inconvenient times because, deep down, I want him to? Or because I haven't yet broken that pattern? I've been doing a pretty good job of not thinking about him throughout this process. Aside from when I've heard from him, obviously. I'll admit that every now and then the question has crossed my mind of whether or not I'll hear from him after Easter. But in that same thought process, I've thought about how I finally feel like I'm close to being over him. Like I could sit across from him a different person, a stronger person, who wouldn't fall back into his charm... or is dicksand the right word for this, too? Why then have I seemingly manifested him in my life on the day before I explore feelings with someone else?

I was listening to something this morning that made an interesting point—we oftentimes wrongfully believe that we are the sum total of our beliefs, values, and experiences. But really, we are the creators. If I'm the creator of my beliefs, then I get to choose the answers to the questions above. And while that's great, I have no idea how to do that. I don't know what I think or feel or believe about Shane.

Dear gut, speak up....

I want to be with Shane.

It's a thought... or a feeling... or I don't even know what, but it's deep inside of me. When I sit and ask myself those questions, that is the answer. That's always been the answer. And part of me hates that it's the answer because I'm afraid it's the wrong answer (fear of failure). And I'm embarrassed it's the answer (my second head).

And how can I trust that answer? What if it is just my mind repeating the same loop it's been playing since I met him? And maybe Ryan is the new path—the path to the life I intentionally *want* and not the life I've been walking blindly towards.

My head is spinning. I have my gut saying I want to be with Shane (who I don't even know if I will ever hear from again), and I have a man I barely know coming to my home tomorrow. And Lent isn't even over!

What am I doing?

JOURNAL ENTRY: promises, promises

APRIL 2017

Well, Ryan is officially on his way. He will be here in less than two hours. I'm mostly nervous but trying to be excited. Our communication this past week has been solely via text. Which is fine with me because I don't really like talking on the phone. It hasn't exactly been lighthearted get-to-know-you texting though— it's been mostly deep, which I know I said is one of the things I like about him. But there were also a couple of occasions where it reminded me of first love Lloyd and the constant "are you okay" questioning, fearing the other person is mad at you. I'll admit it hasn't really been fun texting. I don't think I've laughed once. But I'm trying not to overthink any of it, understanding that it's easy to misread texts from someone you don't know very well.

Bottom line—I'm determined to keep an open mind.

I really don't want to dismiss this situation for *any* reason other than not being into him.

I do feel a little guilty though that it's still Lent and I'm having a man (which I gave up) come visit me. I was listening to a podcast earlier today when I was cleaning my apartment; it was talking about the importance of keeping your word, both to others and to yourself. Keeping promises to yourself is important in order to have a good relationship with yourself. It sounded an awful lot like my conversation with Ronin on the beach in Coco Cay. I haven't exactly kept my Lenten promises to myself—I drank vodka one night on the cruise, I allowed the flirtation (and kiss) to happen with Ryan, and now he's coming to stay with me for a night. Have I broken my word to myself? Or had I not entertained this connection, would that have been me living too far to one extreme? I probably shouldn't have kissed him. I should have given him my number and told him to contact me after Easter. That would have been keeping my word to myself.

Ugh. Too late now. I guess I failed the third test the universe threw at me. Double ugh. (Or I guess triple ugh.)

JOURNAL ENTRY: I have risen, *part 1*

APRIL 2017

Alright. It's Easter evening. Lent is officially over. I ate two delicious cake pops earlier, checked Instagram, had a liquor drink last night, and woke up next to a man.

I'm still processing the night with Ryan. When he first got to my place, he was sweet, complimentary, and relatively open. As the night went on, he would swing back and forth between displaying that open, playful side and showing a quieter, sadder, almost darker side. I reacted quickly to both—when he was open and playful, I relaxed, got out of my head, and tried (admittedly too hard) to have fun. When he turned quiet and dark, I got nervous and analytical. I would catch myself in that state, realize I didn't like it, and try to lighten the mood.

Not exactly a relaxing evening.

Now that I know more about him, the ping pong between moods doesn't surprise me. When we met on the cruise, I didn't know the extent of his career in the military. I know more now but still not everything. Basically, he was a kid who saw and did some horrible things. It was his job and he was good at it. It was his contribution, his self-worth... and then a bomb quickly and suddenly took it away from him and he was thrust back into a "normal" life with a slightly broken body and very broken spirit. He wants to be happy. He wants to find a purpose and joy in this new life... but he can't yet seem to fully escape where he's been and the seemingly pointless nature of his current days. Those are his mood swings. He goes from living in the moment to questioning the point of the moment.

Luna—if you're reading this, you were right.

Out of all the complicated men I've known, he is by far the most complicated. How ironic that he comes into my life right when I'm trying to change my mindset which has attracted such complicated, closed-off men.

I still don't know what to do. There were moments

where he was sweet and I just wanted to hold him and help him through everything. Is that a flaw of mine or is that me living my purpose? Make life better. I could make his life better. Just like I wanted to make Charlie's life better, and Shane's life better. They didn't let me and maybe Ryan will. I assume the lesson here lies somewhere along the lines of finding the balance—of course—between living my purpose in regard to others and also myself.

To make someone else's life better and by being with that person, my life is better as well. I don't know where Ryan stands with that yet. I feel some kind of draw to him. But I'm also afraid that draw is a product of my old ways—that draw is really just me enjoying the feeling of being wanted.

My gut is telling me it's the latter. It did not feel easy to be with Ryan. I did not feel relaxed and comfortable in my own skin. And it wasn't the exciting new love type of nerves I felt. It was more the discomfort that comes with forcing something; the discomfort that comes with not being true to yourself... a discomfort I'm now more aware of because I've lived it for so long.

I'm not looking forward to having this conversation with Ryan—how do I possibly explain all this to him? Or do I just do the typical "it's not you, it's me" excuse? Ironically, that statement is kinda true... it's just a **VERY** extreme simplification.

JOURNAL ENTRY: I have risen, *part 2*

APRIL 2017

When I reflect on the past forty-something days and all the relationships that led me to the point of giving up men for Lent, I realize I've spent so much time feeling sorry for myself. Oh woe is me that the men I loved never chose me—first love Lloyd chose Danielle over me, Arlo chose not to change his life so I could be a real part of it, Charlie chose to go back to his wife, and Shane chose to disappear... and then disappear again. Wah, wah, wah. But now I realize—how could I expect them to choose me when I wasn't even choosing me?

I lost myself... either I was too focused on what other people thought/wanted for my life, or I was drowning in dicksand... or alcohol. Either way, I was always lost on some level. I wasn't being true to me. So either those men fell in love with a "me" who wasn't really me—which clearly means that our relationship wouldn't (and shouldn't) last—or maybe they fell in love with the real me only to realize she wasn't actually around all that much. She always got buried under other priorities. Well, not anymore.

I have a new sense of ownership over my life. I'm not the victim. I've been my own villain. Take the whole history with Lloyd—I always threw myself a little pity party that we didn't end up together, as was my plan. But looking back on it, I'm the one who effed it up. I stood strong in breaking up before our sophomore year of college so I could have the college experience I was "supposed to have"—so essentially I chose the bar and getting drunk over him. It was like I sold a piece of my soul to be cool. Then I was too drunk to remember our phone conversation after I ran into him at the hole-in-the-wall bar by my parents' house… and I chose not to deal with it, not to follow up, not to try to figure out what was said. I chose instead to escape back to school where I was comfortable and accepted… where there was little risk of rejection.

And Arlo—I ignored red flag after red flag. Why? Maybe on some level I was rebelling from having given up Lloyd so easily and therefore I was determined to stand my ground in my relationship with Arlo. Only problem was, it wasn't solid ground. It was dicksand.

Don't even get me started with Charlie—who knowingly gets into a relationship with a married man and actually expects "love to conquer all"? A villain of her own happiness. A freaking masochist, that's who.

And Shane... I haven't quite figured that one out yet. Maybe because that story hasn't ended.

I see now that these past 40-ish days are only the beginning. This process of identifying and staying true to who I really am will continue forever. Because it was never really about men, or drinking, or any other distraction—it was and will always be about me. Me living *my* life... being true to myself and pursuing what I want out of life, despite what anyone else thinks. Just like getting off track was a slow progression, so will be getting back on track. I will need to live and relive these realizations I've made about my purpose and the life I want over and over again. It will be a constant process of growth.

But as with the Fibonacci spiral, I had to go from zero to one. I had to take the first step. Giving up men and the other distractions was necessary for that first step to happen... it cleared the path. And now

I know the only one who can stand in the way of the next step and the next step is me. I control my life... for better or worse.

I by no means have it all figured out. But I also know this—there is no turning back. I feel a change in me that will not allow a total relapse. I'm sure I will have setbacks along the way—like I already have—but there is something in me now that will not settle back into the life I was living.

I fear the road ahead will get bumpy as the people in my life realize I'm not turning back; I'm not in a phase. Today when I declined a glass of wine at my parents' house, my mother jokingly said to my cousin that I'm "kind of a prude now." If I called her out on that comment, she would feel horrible and apologize. Instead I just let it ride (as Ryan would say). I know people will continue to question me, the changes I've made, and my future life choices. But what this whole experience has taught me is that the only questions about me and my life choices which matter are the ones that I ask.

And if there is one thing I hope you take away from this book, it is to do the same—to question your life. Question your choices. Ask your "whys." Make sure your answers are yours.

In just forty-something days, I realized life was much bigger than I was living it. I defined goals and set new expectations. I started to explore questions about my long-held beliefs and habits. I realized I was off track and started taking steps to get back on the path... on *my* path.

Maybe this book will be published and maybe it won't. But I'm writing it. And in September, I'll be flying to Africa... to make a difference. And that's just the beginning.

And as far as the distractions I so hate to love... *What will come of my relationship with alcohol? Is there more to me and David than friendship? Will I hear from Shane tomorrow?*

...I guess we'll see what the next forty days bring.

CONNECT WITH ME

Instagram @kaciemain_write

Facebook @kaciemain.write

Twitter @kaciemain_write

LinkedIn @Kacie Main

YouTube @Kacie Main

www.kaciemain.com

MY THANK YOUS

I am beyond grateful for my publisher, Ben Allen, for taking a chance on me. Published memoirs are typically written by someone who is famous or has overcome a dramatic or unique situation. I am neither of those things. I'm a normal person living a normal life. But Ben saw the importance and potential power in sharing real life stories and I'm so thankful he believed in mine.

Another enormous thank you to Jennifer Collins, my editor, who I also now see as my therapist. As a rookie at this, I was under the impression that once my manuscript got into the hands of a real editor, I was done. She would fix it for me. Man was I wrong! That's when the real work started. She pushed me to go deeper and further with this book than I would have ever gone on my own. But like any great teacher, she never gave me the answers... she just asked all the right questions.

I would not have been able to do this without the support of my family, who I know at times struggled with the idea of me putting so much of our life out into the world. Their love for me is the greatest definition of love—understanding and unending. There are no words to express my gratitude for them.

Thank you to all my soul mate friends throughout the years—the sixpack, mo anam cara, core four, ladies league, table makin', sunrise Sunday crew. These incredible women were always there for me, whether I leaned on them or not. They loved me when the men in my life didn't; they loved me when I didn't love myself. They helped keep me afloat through every storm.

And to my best cheering squad—a group of inspiring women we've named FEATT (Female Entrepreneurial Artistic Think Tank). I'm not sure I would have had the courage to keep pressing forward without them. They read the very first—and very rough—draft of this book. Their excitement about it and their connection to it gave me the validation I needed at the time to keep moving forward.

I'm also very grateful for my personal trainer and his unique love of working out to motivational videos. Had it not been for him, I may have never stumbled across the "what is your purpose" YouTube video that forever changed my life.

To Hadley's dad, pen name Ocean Palmer, thank you for teaching me that my one head was actually three. That blew my mind(s) and opened my world.

Most importantly, to everyone who has accepted and embraced the "new" me... from the bottom of my heart—thank you. This has been a tough road at times... a lonely road at times. I've experienced the full range of emotions—from complete excitement to total fear. But every time I opened up a little bit more... revealing more of who I really am... and you accepted me... and still loved me... I feared a little less and was able to love a little more.

To the people in my life who do not understand what's going on with me... or who don't approve... I get it. My hope is that one day you will. My hope is that one day we will reconnect. And if that day never comes, I will still cherish the memories we have made, and still smile every time I think of you.

And last but not least—thank you to you, whoever you are, for reading my story.

52598117R00220

Made in the USA
Columbia, SC
05 March 2019